CRIMINAL LIVERPOOL

Daniel K. Longman

For the mates, past and present

With special thanks to

Sabrina Chengalanee

Joy Dean

Martin Edwards

Rosalie Spire

First published 2008

Reprinted 2012

The History Press
The Mill, Brimscombe Port
Stroud, Gloucestershire, GL5 2QG
www.thehistorypress.co.uk

© Daniel K. Longman, 2008

The right of Daniel K. Longman to be identified as the Author of this work has been asserted in accordance with the Copyrights, Designs and Patents Act 1988.

All rights reserved. No part of this book may be reprinted or reproduced or utilised in any form or by any electronic, mechanical or other means, now known or hereafter invented, including photocopying and recording, or in any information storage or retrieval system, without the permission in writing from the Publishers.

British Library Cataloguing in Publication Data.
A catalogue record for this book is available from the British Library.

ISBN 978 0 7509 4749 7

Typesetting and origination by The History Press.
Printed in Great Britain

CONTENTS

Foreword by Martin Edwards   4
Introduction   6

With a View to Matrimony	9
The Toxteth Tot	14
Family Ties	17
A Heated Argument	26
Revenge of a Pimp	31
A Suspicious Son-In-Law	37
A Charred Concealment	40
The Solicitor Shooting	44
The Wrong Class	49
Depression of a Corn Dealer	52
Nudity at Lancelot's Hey	56
Mistranscriptions	60
A Day at the Dentist	64
Mysterious Circumstances	67
The Bully	71
A Fiery Feline	77
The Die-hard Marketers	80
A Bit on the Side	83
Tragedy at Upholland	85
Coppers in the Dock	87
The Pact	89
Death of a Sweetheart	92
Madam Brennan	96
A Measurable Offence	99
A Question of Sanity	101
A Remarkable Capture	106
The Chocolate Box	108
The Mummy of Hope Place	111
An Unfortunate Hurry	114
No. 22 Mount Pleasant	116
Nurse Jones	119

Index   127

FOREWORD

There are plenty of true stories about crime in Liverpool, as well as plenty of jokes. There is also a good deal of misunderstanding about it – statistics suggest that there is rather less crime on Merseyside than in various other parts of the country. But inevitably, such a rugged city has seen many crimes committed in its 800 years of history, and this book gathers together a variety of stories recounting them. The cases include murder, naturally, but also encompass other felonies.

One story to be found in these pages that I had never heard before concerns the solicitor James Wilcox Alsop. He was a member of a distinguished law firm and, although the tale dates back to 1908, the name of Alsop, Stevens was still pre-eminent in the city's legal profession when I started out on my career as a solicitor – they occupied offices in India Buildings, a stone's throw from where I work to this day, more than seventy years later. And although his story falls outside the scope of this book, Herbert Rowse Armstrong, 'the Hay Poisoner', said to be the only English solicitor ever to be hanged – but by no means the only solicitor to have killed someone – worked for Alsop, Stevens. He moved to Hay-on-Wye only a couple of years or so before the attack on Mr Alsop.

Once I had settled to working life in Liverpool, it struck me that, if I were to pursue my ambition of writing a series of crime novels, I could do much worse than set it in the city. I discovered that despite all that is said about the prevalence of crime in Liverpool, no fictional crime series had ever been located there. There had been occasional crime novels set wholly or partly in Merseyside – indeed, Hercule Poirot makes a trip to the city in Agatha Christie's classic whodunit *The Murder of Roger Ackroyd* – but detective novelists traditionally favoured genteel settings, such as Oxford colleges, for their mysteries. This seemed strange to me, and I created a fictional Liverpool lawyer, Harry Devlin, to detect the criminal puzzles that I devised. Seventeen years after his first appearance, he continues to walk the city's mean streets, though after so much regeneration they are rather less mean than they used to be.

It would, though, be hard for any crime novelist to top real life, when one bears in mind that Liverpool has provided the backdrop for two of the most famous murder mysteries of all time – I refer to the Maybrick and Wallace cases, which have fascinated generations of students of true crime, as well as such legendary detective novelists as Raymond Chandler, Dorothy L. Sayers, and Anthony Berkeley. The Maybrick case took an extraordinary turn in the 1980s, with the discovery of a diary, purporting to give the confession of James Maybrick (previously known as the famous victim of a Victorian arsenical poisoning) to the Jack the Ripper murders. If the diary is a hoax, it is an ingenious one. Any mystery novelist would have been proud to have dreamed up that particular twist.

Wisely, Daniel Longman has resisted any temptation to re-hash well-worn material, and has come up with a wide range of cases which will be unfamiliar even to seasoned readers of real-life cases. A capacity for research and a willingness to focus on fresh material are two important ingredients of success for any true crime writer; Daniel at nineteen is, as far as I know, the youngest specialist in true crime in Britain, but his industry and the breadth of scope of his writing augur well for the future. The recent death of Jonathan Goodman – who worked in Liverpool in the 1960s and who made his name with a famous study of the Wallace case – robbed us of an acknowledged master of the true-crime genre. One would like to think that, in Daniel Longman, we have someone whose researches will, in the fullness of time, achieve as much attention as did the late Jonathan Goodman's.

Martin Edwards
www.martinedwardsbooks.com

INTRODUCTION

The year 2008 has seen Liverpool celebrate its coronation as Europe's Capital of Culture. This accolade made interesting reading to many, not least to the residents and businessmen from those cities that narrowly missed out on the desirable title. Liverpool is undergoing massive aesthetic change, granting many parts of the city a much-needed face-lift; a procedure which it cannot be denied she desperately needs. At the start of the year local media reports teased us with a spectacular list of events that lay flirtatiously in wait. The area's papers went absolutely giddy for 2008 and any eager reader would have been hard-pressed to find an article unconnected with the recent revelry. Merseyside's radio airwaves became swamped with the same hearty hullabaloo leaving no one in any doubt that this year was Liverpool's year.

Fun, music, glamour and, of course, culture were supposed to spill out onto the soon-to-be tourist-packed streets creating a haven of chic modern living in this once ailing and desperate shipping town. Towering cranes lined every street corner carefully constructing buildings that would hopefully climb to the clouds. Hotels, restaurants, bars and more sprang up like concrete daisies with the intention of creating a vast number of jobs and boosting the country's economy. Famous children of the city, many of whom had not returned since leaving all those years ago, have made an exultant return, eager to be seen singing the city's praises. Colourful flags blew cheerily on Liverpool's pavements, huge purple posters covered the sides of whole buildings and commercialised Scouse excitement was virtually forced upon you.

It was crucial that Liverpool made the most of this year. It is a rare treat for a town to be given so much coverage and to be inundated with so much tourism. We were told that thousands – if not millions – of visitors will continue to flock to the city in search of cultural satisfaction and our job is to meet those hungry cravings. The fantastically educational World Museum stands grandly in William Brown Street, packed full of fascinating artefacts and exhibits. Next door lies the Walker Gallery, a building that boasts some of the finest artwork

INTRODUCTION

Liverpool Magistrates Court in Dale Street, where today's delinquents are dealt with.

on the planet. Take a stroll through the centralised gardens and you shall find, quite easily, St George's Hall, an incredible piece of Victorian architecture and one of the most recognisable buildings in the country. The Albert Dock, with the fabulous Tate, draws many a critic to walk its cobbled paths to muse on creation. You can't forget about the music, even if you wanted to. Whatever your tastes, nobody can deny that some of the world's most revered musicians hail from these streets. The Beatles Museum has become a place of pilgrimage for many a die-hard fan. However hard you try you cannot escape the Fab Four's influence, even forty years on.

A recent addition to Merseyside's culture checklist is the International Slavery Museum. Inside people can discover some of Liverpool's more notorious heritage and reflect on exactly how the town's abundant Georgian wealth was actually achieved. The history of this city is long and varied. Some is commendable; some is, perhaps, not so praiseworthy. Hopefully I can play my small part by relaying some of Liverpool's historic past, even if it is slightly unsavoury, in this book.

Liverpool has never truly been any different to any other big city in terms of crime levels, and, despite the thankfully dying stereotype, the town is actually quite a safe place to be. Today the outdated view that the town is particularly dangerous just doesn't ring true. From London to Manchester, Newcastle to Bristol, crime happens; it's just a sad fact of life.

Assaults and injuries have always been a possibility. As this book will relate, murders, robberies, beatings, etc have existed since time immemorial: the only difference is the manner in which they were carried out and reported. Despite well-intentioned Government policy the police are still working flat out to curb illegality. Gangs are still managing to obtain weapons with what seems a relative ease and there is no sign of a letup. Things have transformed though: what was once the humble knife has become the automatic firearm. What was once a careless equestrian accident is now a callous hit and run. What was once a carefully planned bank hold-up is now faceless internet fraud. Crime and the ability to fight crime are constantly evolving, taking on new forms and disguises. Yet if history has taught us anything it is that the world shall never be free of it. It would be foolish to believe any city, even Liverpool, could prove otherwise and criminals, however cultured they now may be, shall continue to thrive within the shady underworld of scandal. We must continue to tackle such delinquency, not only in this city but across the whole nation.

The year 2008 has finally put Liverpool back on the map and this time for the right reasons. I predict that this year shall be remembered as the year this city turned itself around and successfully shed the old-fashioned, detrimental and stereotypical image that has a hung around her neck for so long.

But until that day, read on and investigate the eyebrow-raising antics of an alleged Lime Street brothel, the shocking shooting of a Scouse solicitor and the barbaric burning of a poor infant.

Daniel K. Longman

WITH A VIEW TO MATRIMONY

Rose Griffiths was a shy and demure domestic servant from Liverpool. In the year 1905, she travelled across to West Kirby to begin new employment as a maid. Rose was an intelligent woman and enjoyed reading the newspapers of her home town. One afternoon, Miss Griffiths was casually scanning the broadsheets when an unusual notice caught her eye.

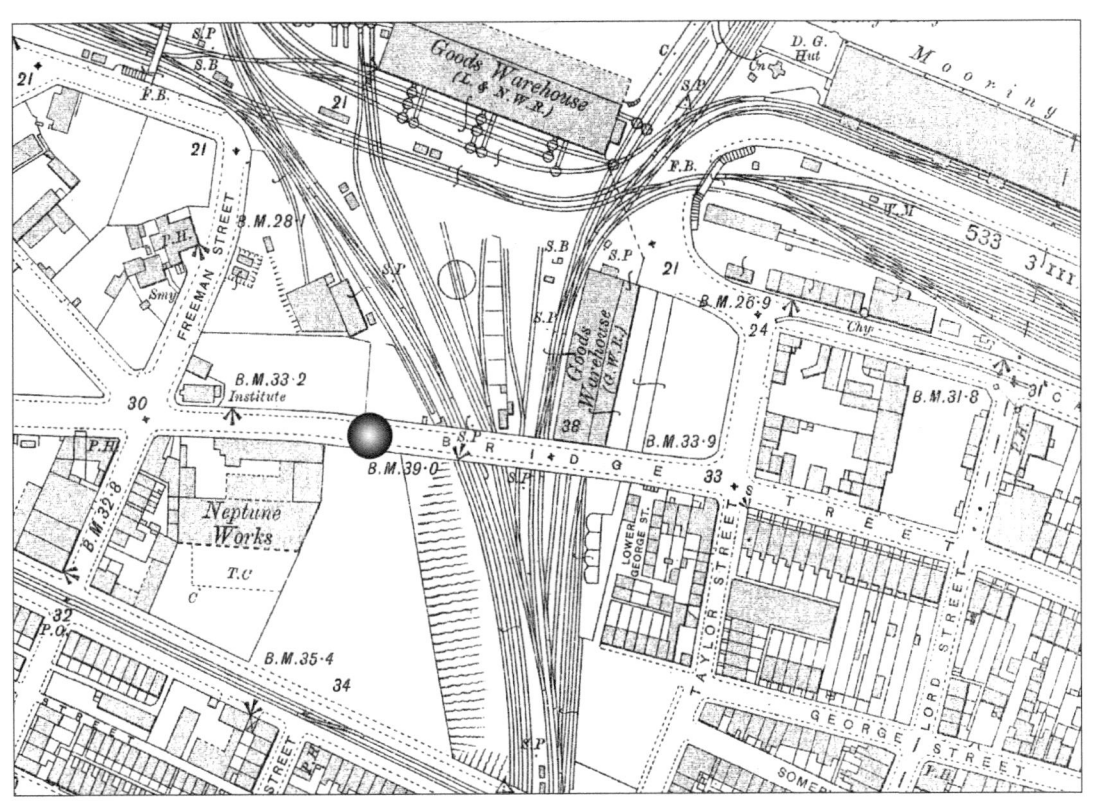

A Victorian map of Bridge Street in Birkenhead, showing the location of the Church Army Home

It was an advertisement, a rather sweet one at that, from a young man wishing to become acquainted with a woman of similar age in the hope of a possible marriage. Rose was intrigued. She was single and had not had much luck with the game of courtship. The advertisement further stated that this lonely bachelor was an electrician earning 3 guineas and 3s a week and was currently staying at the Church Army Home in Bridge Street, Birkenhead. On 22 November, Rose eagerly penned a letter in answer to the advert, enclosing her 'Girl's Friendly Society' card, and was thrilled to receive a swift reply:

> Referring to your answer to my advertisement, for which I thank you, I will in confidence give you a few particulars of myself. I wish you to clearly understand that my advert is genuine and honourable and would be pleased to hear from you. I am an electrical engineer and on the engineering staff on the electric light company here, where I have been since my father's death.

Rose's interest in Frederick Ward, her new pen pal, increased, and she was pleased to read further of his well-furnished home in Seacombe. Mr Ward also mentioned that he earned a little bit extra by holding the saintly job of organist at Holy Trinity Church and was also an avid member of several societies.

The smitten maid wrote back, but for several days heard no reply. She decided to pay Frederick a surprise visit and went along to the Church Army Home in the hope of finding him. To his utter shock Mr Ward was approached by the young woman and was immediately questioned.

'Are you Mr Ward?' Rose asked politely.

'Erm, yes,' answered the man hesitantly. 'I'm sorry for not replying. I have been working late.' He said that she would have to go as he was still working and followed her to the door. Frederick did however wish to speak with Rose again and made arrangements for the two of them to go out the following Saturday night.

The date went as well as could be hoped and as the evening went on Rose became even more infatuated with the charming Mr Ward. As the pair walked along the moonlit streets, the evening's conversation turned to the future, and Mr Ward spoke of how he had been left quite a quantity of furniture in his mother's will and was planning to set up a home. He sweetly asked Miss Griffiths if she would be interested in starting it with him. Rose couldn't help but smile and her stomach filled with butterflies. Frederick told her how he owned a house on the promenade at Seacombe but was currently renting it out. 'It's called 'Rose-Lea,' said Fred, and from his pocket he produced an ivy leaf, plucked from the very wall of the cottage itself. Rose was only too happy to say yes to the proposal and ecstatically threw her arms round her new fiancé. The pair continued to meet and exchange affectionate letters for some time, one in which Mr Ward wrote, 'I would only be too proud to make you my wife.' Rose was overjoyed at the prospect and said that she would do anything that she could to make their dream a reality. Not long afterwards Rose received another letter from her beau. It read:

> Now I have started with our home, and little expenses will keep coming, but it must be done now. My brother-in-law will help me with a few pounds on the 21st November. Do you think you could help me a little more? I'm sorry to trouble you, my loved one. I promise to share all with you. You shall have a nice present.

In December Frederick asked her to come over to see him as he wished to see her cheerful face as he was feeling low spirited. The pair met and went for a walk, during which the electrician told Rose that he had been having some money troubles. He had incurred some doctor's expenses and had been sent a larger-than-expected invoice by the company storing his dead mother's furniture. He asked Rose if she could help him out.

'I'll pay you back when I get my quarter salary for playing the organ,' he promised.

For the first time, a sense of suspicion overcame Rose and she began to wonder why she, a mere domestic servant, had to help someone who had two jobs and a rental income. 'So how much will you be getting then, Fred?' asked the young maid inquisitively.

He said that the Holy Trinity Church paid him £25 a year. Not only did he again promise to pay back the money, Frederick reverted back to the house at Seacombe and reminded Rose he was in the process of getting it ready for them both so that they could start living happily ever after. It would have electric lighting throughout and even a telephone!

Rose was once again blinded by Mr Ward's wonderfully idyllic words and his verbal painting of what would soon be her life swept away any misgivings she may have had about her fabulous fiancé. Later that month Rose had a change of situation and began working at a house in Seaforth. On Boxing Night she met her ardent lover and handed him 15s while walking to Liverpool. A week later Rose gave Frederick a further £1, but made it clear to him that she had no more savings or disposable income. Fred felt guilty. He reached into his pocket and gave her 11d. The marriage he had promised

Bridge Street, Birkenhead in 2008, the site of Frederick Ward's 'residence'.

was still on course and was set for February. He professed that the curate at their marriage ceremony was to be the same man who officiated over his sister's nuptials, and the cottage was almost ready for them to move into. Furthermore, Frederick's employer was apparently planning to promote him, meaning a better wage and better hours. All this, he claimed, was to be just the start of a wonderful life for them both.

They arranged to meet later in the week at College Road, Seaforth. With a warm embrace, the couple parted with a kiss. That was to be the last time the beautiful Rose Griffiths would ever see the audacious Mr Ward. She arrived at College Road as planned, and waited. Time passed and Fred was nowhere to be seen. A tear crept down Rose's cheek as the painful realisation of how stupid she had been finally hit her. She had been duped.

She made enquiries at the Church Army Home as to the whereabouts of the wicked absconder, but could only find a smouldering trail of his lies. Joseph

Davies, captain of the home, told the Liverpool lady that the man she was looking for came to him on 11 November 1905, and, as far as Mr Davies knew, had previously been a confectioner in Dewsbury, West Yorkshire. He also stated that Frederick mentioned something about working with a cousin in Belfast and had left, possibly to go there. The inmates of the home worshipped at Holy Trinity, but the organist certainly hadn't been Frederick Ward. In fact, Frederick was paid 8s a week for chopping sticks.

The case was taken to court and on 13 September, the runaway husband-to-be was tracked down and forced to stand trial before magistrates. Evidence from Rose Griffiths and Mr Davies was heard, as well as from a book keeper from a Liverpool furniture company. He stated that the prisoner had ordered no services from the company and – contrary to his claims – that they had never stored any items belonging to him at all. Detective Sergeant Mountfield deposed that he had received Mr Ward from the Stockport police where, it seems, he was trying to commit similar crimes. Indeed, both the Liverpool and Norwich constabularies had a warrant out for Frederick's arrest for past attempts at matrimonial deception. On investigation it was discovered that even the dream cottage, 'Rose-Lea', did not exist. Frederick did not try to defend himself but stood in the dock calmly, seemingly oblivious to the upset that his crimes had caused. The charge against him (that of obtaining money through false pretences) was deemed too severe for a police court, so the prisoner was sent to the sessions. It was there that he was found guilty by the deputy recorder, who took a very serious view of the case. It was decided that Frederick Ward would be sent to prison for twelve months with hard labour in the hope of persuading him to give up his culpable lifestyle on his eventual release. It is unknown whether the heartbroken Rose Griffiths went on to find a true, honest love.

THE TOXTETH TOT

On 30 January 1893, the county coroner, Mr Brighouse, held an inquest into the rather gruesome discovery made by two local lads. It was heard that at midday the previous Friday, fourteen-year-old Alexander Browne and his friend Reginald McGeorge had been playing on some wasteland in Marmion Road, Toxteth Park. The two boys were happily playing in the fresh air when Reginald's attention was suddenly caught by something unusual in the mud. The friends decided to take a closer look.

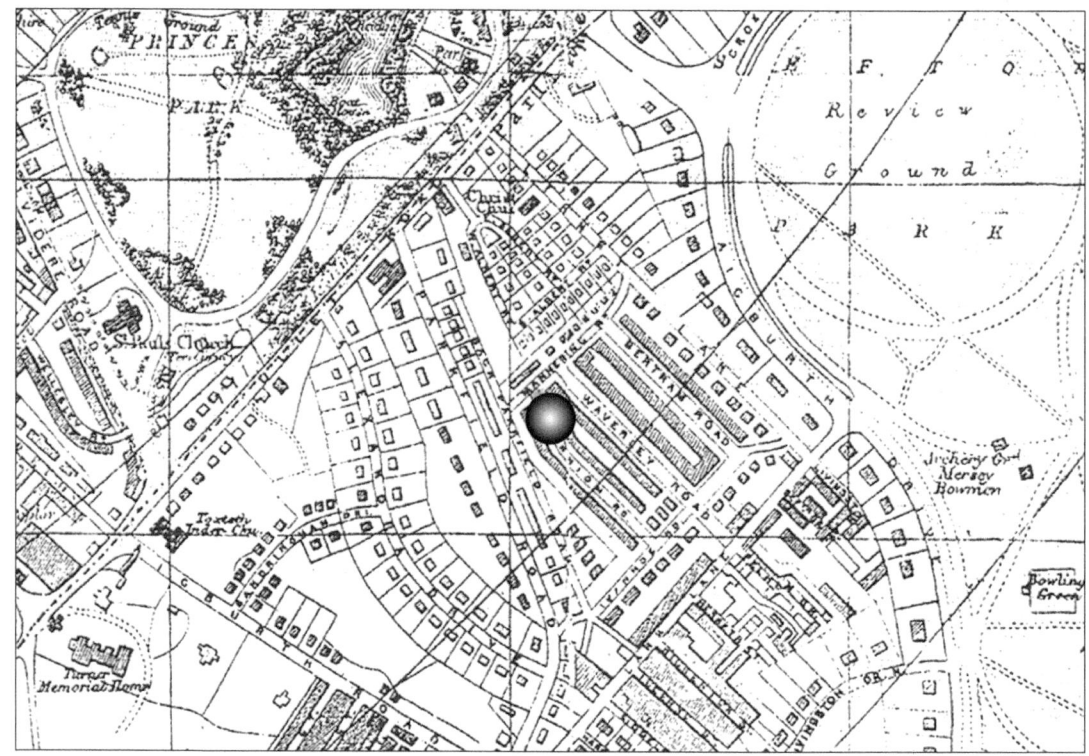

Marmion Road, Toxteth Park in 1901.

Marmion Road, Toxteth Park as it appears in 2008.

The curiosity that lay before them was round and stumpy, not unlike a turnip. Keen to find out exactly what it was, Alex and Reggie beckoned a passing butcher boy and asked for his opinion on their bizarre find. The apprentice knelt down and peered into the ground. It did not take long for a sick sense of realisation to overcome him and the boy fell back in horror. The half-buried globular mass was no turnip. It was a head!

Sergeant Foster was contacted by the trio and he and a constable headed to Toxteth Park to investigate the lads' revolting claims. There in the waste ground sat the head, hidden in a dirt hole approximately 1ft deep. Its features were unrecognisable due to the natural decomposition and weathering that had obviously taken place. Nevertheless, it was clear that this was the head of a young child. Not far from the head lay several pieces of burnt canvas and, on inspecting the blackened materials, Sergeant Foster and his colleague found more remains of the body: the back of the abdomen, the tiny left leg and several other body parts were all strewn about the area. Despite a thorough search, the right leg, the chest and one of the arms could not be located. From what could be found, the two men were left in no doubt that this was the corpse of a very young child.

Nine-year-old Reginald, of 12 Ivanhoe Road, told the court that he could recall witnessing some boys playing with a fire on the wasteland one day in December, but had thought nothing of it.

Margaret Joyce, a domestic servant from 35 Marmion Road, attested that she, also, could remember seeing a small fire burning in the exact location in question about month previously and that it had smouldered for the greater portion of the day.

Dr Oliver of Lark Lane stated that he had examined the remains and from the unusually hard state of the charred bones was of the opinion that the child was between three and six months old. He also believed that the remains had been in the ground for approximately five or six weeks, but pointed out that the missing parts would not have been destroyed by fire and would not have decomposed so rapidly. The doctor could offer no explanation as to the cause of death.

The jury retuned an open verdict; neither the identity of the baby nor the circumstances surrounding its repulsive fate were ever discovered.

FAMILY TIES

In the year 1877, forty-five-year-old Elizabeth Kirkbride lodged at a small and unremarkable house in the suburb of Tuebrook, West Derby. With the help of her two sons she was able to earn a paltry living selling her skills in fancy needlework. Things had changed considerably for Elizabeth, who had been a schoolmistress for a number of years in the village of Lonworthby in Penrith. The daughter of a customs surveyor, she had been born in Liverpool

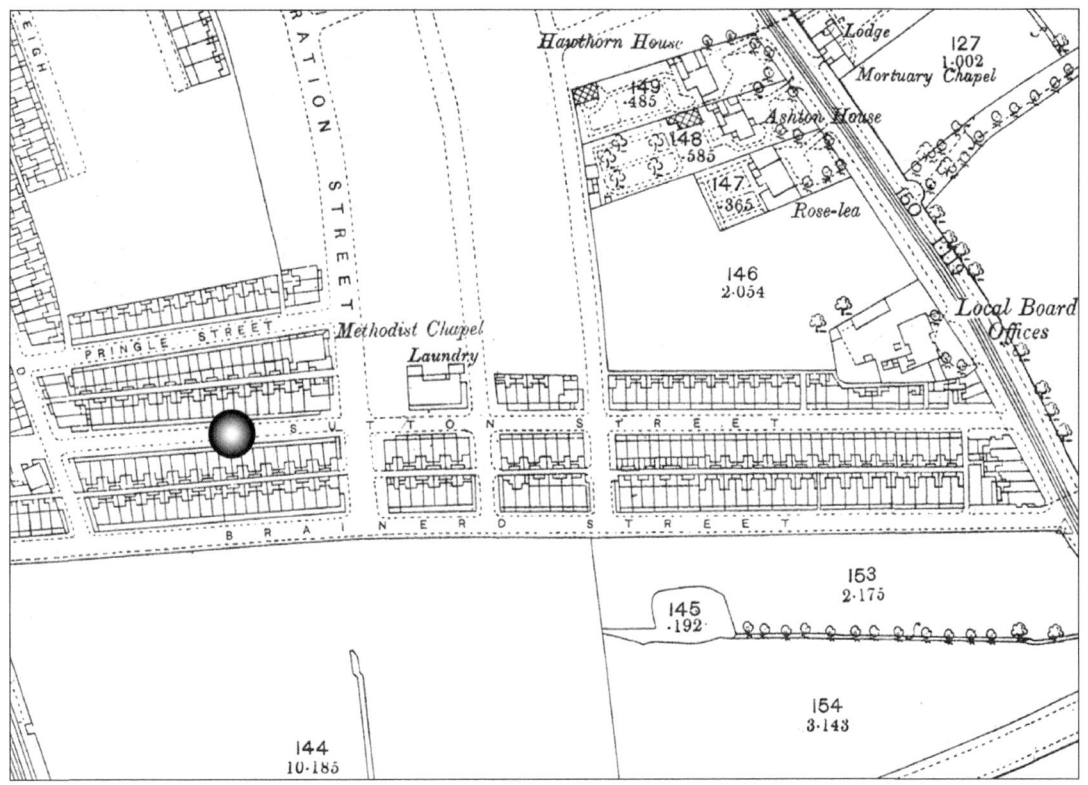

Sutton Street, Tuebrook as depicted in 1893.

Elizabeth Kirkbride's lodgings in Sutton Street, Tuebrook.

and was an only child. She had received a high standard of education and one of her many accomplishments was fluency in several languages. The middle-aged woman had once enjoyed a relatively comfortable lifestyle but an unfortunate change of circumstance brought all of that to an end. Elizabeth's husband, a government collector of reformatory fees, passed away, leaving her widowed. She moved away from Penrith to live with her parents in Helton, Westmoreland and to start her life again.

Years passed, and Elizabeth once again found herself settled in Liverpool and struggling to earn a wage. In the month of January 1877, Mrs Kirkbride's life was thrown into turmoil. At six o'clock on Sunday the 29th, Sergeant Robinson arrived at her lodgings, 21 Sutton Street, and informed her that he had a warrant for her arrest.

'I am charging you with the concealment of child birth at Penrith,' he told her. Elizabeth seemed confused and stated that there must be some sort of mistake.

She made no attempt to get ready, forcing the officer to repeat his instructions.

'Could you put on your shawl and bonnet, Mrs Kirkbride?' asked Sergeant Robinson. This she did, but first Elizabeth asked if she could write a note to her sons explaining the situation; they were asleep upstairs and she did not wish to disturb them. Once this was done, the officer escorted the bewildered woman away for questioning.

She was told that the previous week a body had been discovered in a box at the Griffin Inn, Penrith, where Mrs Kirkbride had stayed some months previously. Staff at the premises found the box left by the woman and stored it away, expecting her to call to collect it. After some time and with still no news, employees began to notice a malodorous and sickly scent emanating from the lumber room where the item was being held. The decision was made to open the mysterious bundle and at once the cause of the odour became clear: a body, that of a small child, lay crooked and deformed under several layers of discoloured material. Staff recoiled in shock at the sight of the tiny corpse. A clean red slash was clearly visible across its minuscule neck.

An inquest failed to determine exactly who or what brought the child's short existence to an end, but the investigation did bring to light the remains of a second child which had also been in the box but which staff had failed to notice. This second baby had evidently been dead for a considerably longer period than its presumed sibling and was in a most rancid state of decomposition. This baby had a length of cord or the hem of a garment bound tightly around its throat.

The following morning the Kirkbride sons came down from their room, with their friend. They left quickly as they were late for work and they wanted to avoid their landlady Emma Orbeti who would ask them awkward questions about the outstanding rent payment. Later that day however Mrs Orbeti met John, the elder brother, as he returned home from work and she was told about his mother's note.

'Did she not leave any rent?' enquired the landlady.

'No,' said Mr Kirkbride awkwardly, 'but I'll settle it.'

Mrs Orbeti also explained that she was missing a few items from the house and wondered if he knew what may have happened to them. John replied that he did not, but would find some things to give her as security until his mother returned.

The two of them made their way upstairs so John could rummage around for anything of value. The nineteen-year-old kicked a large heavy box which they had acquired shortly after moving in. The lid fell open and a horrible aroma began to fill the landing. John imagined the cause of the stench to be nothing but old damp clothes, so closed the lid and moved on to another trunk to see what he could find. On the top was a gummed paper label. It read, 'Stockport, Mrs Hayton, Miss Laws, Hazel Grove'.

Alas, this box was shut tight, and Mr Kirkbride could not muster enough strength to open it. He shrugged and repeated that his mother would be back in a few days and that he was sure that the rent would be settled as soon as she returned. The disgruntled landlady accepted that the young man had tried his best and let him go about his business.

Later Mrs Orbeti's curiosity, coupled with her need for the rent, got the better of her. She casually returned to the landing and tried again to crack open the sealed box. A wry smile beamed across her face as the lid loosened. A fearful stench was released. She was not smiling now. Emma put her hand to her mouth and retched. Inside she could see wrappings and sheets that caused alarm bells to ring inside her head. She closed the hellish container and dragged it down the stair. The heartbeat-like thump echoed throughout the property as the troubled woman slowly but surely heaved the trunk down the staircase and out into the backyard.

'Sidney!' she shouted. Her son soon came over to see what the matter was. Emma asked him to investigate the putrid stench and upon opening the coverings an unspeakable sight was revealed.

They closed the box and Mrs Orbeti went to inform the authorities. At Tuebrook police station two officers listened to Emma's concerns and returned to Sutton Street with her to look into the matter. They knelt down to examine the foul-smelling chest and began to unwrap the pieces of carpet and wallpaper. One item appeared to be a small doll covered in rotten rags; the other was obviously a child in a ghastly state of decay. What was in another parcel was falling to pieces but the policemen could see part of the mass was a slice of skull. Superintendent Sheppard shook his head and closed the box tight. He told Mrs Orbeti that he and his colleague would have to take the box to the station for further examination and with that, the two men carried the trunk from the house.

Back in custody Mrs Kirkbride was informed by Superintendent Martin of the additional charge of concealment of three births. In reply she admitted to their concealment and neglect but strongly denied murdering them.

'I made no mention of murder to you, Mrs Kirkbride,' answered Mr Martin.

On the Wednesday morning of 31 January, Elizabeth Kirkbride attended an inquest into the suspicious bodies at her residence in Sutton Street. At the St George's Hotel in Green Lane, evidence was presented by Dr Henry Yates Pitts. He stated that the previous day he and Inspector Walsh had examined the remains of three children in total.

> The first was tolerably perfect. I could not tell whether it was male or female, it was in a state of dry-decay. I next drew out from the trunk a child with no head; this was newborn, fully formed and in a more advanced state of decay than the other. While seeking the child's head I found more bones sufficient for the trunk and limbs of a third infant which may have been in the box for nine or ten years; the other two at distant periods, the last one about four to five years ago.

The jury listened in horror as the physician continued to relay his harrowing findings. 'There was a rag tied about the neck of the child with a head. Comparing the size of the rag to that of the neck of a newborn child it must have been tightly tied. The shrinking of the neck had caused it to come loose,' Dr Pitts stated. 'I can give no idea of the cause of death or whether they were born alive owing to the condition of the bodies.'

John Kirkbride could offer no explanation for the bodies. 'I never had the slightest suspicion that there was anything wrong in the box, nor that my mother was ever in the family way since my father's death.'

'You can not tell whether the children are hers or who the mother is?' questioned the coroner.

'No, sir, I have not the slightest idea.'

The teenager was then questioned about the containers themselves.

'She had the boxes with her when she came from Carlisle station to Aintree in June last and they were left at the latter station until August. Our object in going to Aintree was to stay with friends there, and later in Aughton. My mother's maiden name was Hayton.'

From this the jury could only determine that the children were found dead in an advanced state of decomposition in a box belonging to Mrs Kirkbride. Whether the children were born alive or how they came to their deaths the evidence failed to show. However, it was a case with the gravest suspicion attached, as the most recently born child was discovered to have had a ligature about its neck. If it could be proved that it was tied with a view to compression, proof was needed to show that the child was born alive. The matter would have to be left to a further tribunal before a decision could be made.

On Saturday 3 February, at the County Magistrates Court in Basnett Street, Elizabeth Kirkbride was tried on charges of concealment. Since the inquest it had emerged that another corpse had been discovered at the house where the prisoner had once lived in Helton. The discovery was made after William, one of her sons, remembered his mother burying something at the base of a peach tree in their garden several years ago. This was to be the sixth charge that Elizabeth faced.

When placed in the dock it was clear that the stress of her confinement had taken its toll. She seemed much weaker and older than she had appeared at the inquest just three days previously.

Inspector Walsh, who led the case, reiterated the details from the inquest but recounted to the jury some new information which had only recently come to light. At about 9 p.m. on Thursday, the officer had received a message that Mrs Kirkbride wished to discuss something of great importance. He and two other officers went to the woman's cell to hear what she had to say. Inspector Walsh repeated her words:

> I want to tell you who the father is of all the children I am here about. His name is Thomas Moss, he is a tea, ham and bacon dealer in Askham near Penrith. He is the only man I had ever had anything to do with in any way, and I think it is only right that he is exposed as it is entirely by his own persuasion that I am placed as I am, and he has always promised that he will make me his wife, instead of doing so, when he was in a position he married another.

Superintendent Fowler of the Cumberland Constabulary produced a warrant for the apprehension of Mrs Kirkbride by his fellow officers, and stated that the offences were committed in Westmoreland. He told the court that it was the opinion of the clerk of the peace that Elizabeth should be taken to be tried locally. The prisoner was handed over, and soon Mrs Kirkbride found herself heading for a train at Lime Street with an inquisitive mass of onlookers watching her every step. One or two people attempted to grab the woman but were held back by police reinforcements. Hundreds followed the cab to the station eager to catch a glimpse of the alleged serial child killer. Once Elizabeth was in the carriage the crowds made a rush. They overturned the barriers and charged hard to the side of the train. A porter quickly held up a rug to block the window as the train steadily sped out of the station leaving a swarm of angry spectators jeering on the platform.

At 6 p.m. the locomotive arrived at Penrith. There were large crowds, but no demonstrations took place. Mrs Kirkbride was sullen and appeared indifferent to the intense curiosity displayed towards her.

On Monday she found herself before Magistrate William Harrison, who formally remanded her until the following Saturday. Back in Liverpool, the three babies found in the box were finally buried in Anfield Cemetery. They were placed in a single coffin with no religious ceremony. Saturday soon came and the former teacher again found herself in the dock, this time before three stern-looking magistrates.

Eighteen-year-old William Kirkbride deposed that he was a tailor's apprentice in Brampton, Westmoreland. Since his father's death his mother had been living with his grandmother in Helton. Neither he nor his brothers lived at home, but with their maternal grandmother.

> I was frequently at my mother's house and I have another brother named Alfred. About five or six years ago, me and my brother were cleaning out the loft above the wash-house. We commenced to throw the dirt and stuff into the midden and observed a white bag. It was tied up and I loosened it. I noticed a red flannel petticoat covered in marks and stains amongst rags and other things. I saw a dead child. It was dry and mummified. The fingers and toes were perfected and it had white hair on its head. I threw it in the midden.

Mr Kirkbride also told the court that he had not told his mother, but instead spoke to his grandmother and two aunts the next day. They told him never to speak of what he saw again and not to return to his mother's house.

'I however did return to my mother's house the next day,' William continued, 'and I noticed in the garden something in the ground covered in earth. It was the same child and I threw some more earth over without touching it.'

The young apprentice did not go near that spot again until recently, to show Police Constable Reed the location. Later, several bones were dug up from the site and taken for examination. Some were found to be human. Mr Kirkbride told the court that in February the preceding year, his mother and grandmother left Helton to live in Langwathby. The furniture was taken by a cab and amongst the items was a tin box which sat beside the driver.

Isabella Nicholson stated that she knew the prisoner well and confirmed that she had moved house with her at Candlemas. It was heard that in Langwathby Mrs Kirkbride had attempted to set up a school, but it had been an unsuccessful venture. Miss Nicholson had remained there until

Whitsuntide, then moved to Carlisle. When Mrs Kirkbride's mother died she too moved to Carlisle and Miss Nicholson had helped her unload her possessions, the tin box again being one of them.

Another witness, Robinson Donaldson, said that the prisoner had employed him to drive a vehicle comprising of boxes, china, a hamper and other various items, between Penrith and Langwathby, where he left the objects with the owner of the Griffin Inn, Mr Jameson.

Mr Jameson himself was called as a witness. He confirmed that Mrs Kirkbride had told him at the beginning of June that she had three boxes that needed to be taken care of until she found a home in Liverpool. His wife Grace stored them in the lumber room where they lay undisturbed until 25 January when the festering remains were discovered by domestic servant Isabella Carruthers.

Several more witnesses gave evidence, including a pointsman and a warehouseman, who each recalled seeing the tin box in question. One witness, Mary Forsyth, related that approximately eleven or twelve years previously, she had worked for Mrs Hayton, the prisoner's mother, as a maid at her home in Helston. At the time Mrs Kirkbride ran a school in the village.

'I was twelve-years-old and in service there for about a year. One Sunday evening the prisoner was in bed and she had a child with her. I can't say the age but she could walk. The prisoner was not well and stayed in bed all day. I heard something like the cry of a newborn baby and I told my mother.'

'Do you mean it was the voice of a child other than the one able to walk?' enquired the Chairman.

'I think so,' replied Mary, 'It was a long time ago.'

The Court mused over the facts before the chairman reiterated the charges and asked whether Mrs Kirkbride had anything to say or wished to call a witness. She did not.

The bench were of the opinion that there was sufficient evidence to commit her for trial at the assizes and Mrs Kirkbride was led, weeping copiously, from the dock.

21 February saw Mrs Kirkbride placed before Baron Huddleston at the Appleby Spring Assizes. The charges of concealment were again put to her and she apathetically pleaded her guilt. It was his view that the prisoner should be charged before Mr Justice Manisty and his jury found a true bill in the case.

The following afternoon Elizabeth's long legal torment came to an end. His Lordship addressed her in most severe terms, saying that she had pleaded guilty to the three collective indictments knowing that there was not a shadow of doubt as to the course which she had pursued, and he feared she knew a great deal more.

'Your conduct is almost incredible, the most inhuman that any human being could be guilty of,' Justice Manisty felt moved to add.

Both he and Baron Huddleston had serious doubts whether she ought not to have been tried for murder. It was a case in which he felt the need to pass more than an ordinary sentence. The extreme punishment for concealment was that of two years hard labour, but he sentenced Mrs Kirkbride to nine months for each charge to which she had pleaded guilty, bringing her aggregated sentence to two years and three months hard labour. The prisoner, who showed no emotion, was then removed.

A HEATED ARGUMENT

On 21 March 1893, the Crown Court of the Liverpool Assizes was the scene of the trial of Peter Brannigan. Mr Justice Willis sat at the head of the courtroom while the accused stood ashamedly in the dock. It was on this Tuesday morning that the painful details of Mrs Brannigan's demise would finally be told. On Christmas Eve the previous year, Mary Jane Usher was in her room at No. 2 Court, Brown Street. She was a single woman who made her living by working as a machinist. Miss Usher rented the parlour of the

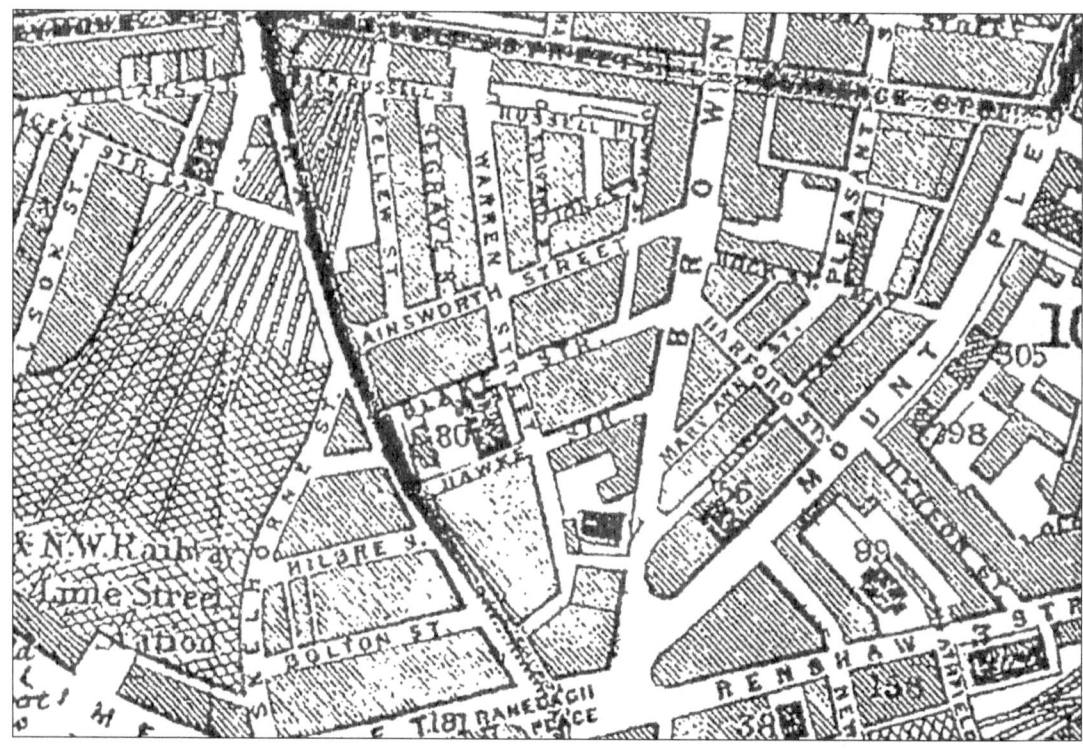

The vicinity of Brown Street as shown on a map from 1891.

The remnants of modern-day Brown Street.

house which she shared with the Brannigans who lived upstairs. She could often hear the couple bickering and arguing; their union was not the best example of marital bliss. Nevertheless, Mary was good friends with Margaret Brannigan and that evening, she was talking with her in the parlour along with another friend, Miss O'Brien. The three ladies had all been drinking and were a little worse for wear. This was certainly the case with Margaret who had to be helped up the stairs to her room.

Later, at about 8.30 p.m., Mrs Brannigan came back downstairs. She was feeling much better but was still very inebriated. It was at this time that forty-year-old Peter Brannigan, her husband, entered the house. He had been drinking as well, but not so freely as Margaret. On seeing the state of his wife his blood began to boil. He rushed towards her, ripped her pocket open and took the few coins she had left. The enraged spouse then lifted his wife up and carried her to their room.

Two hours later, at about 10 p.m., Thomas Quinn, a tenant who resided in the room below the Brannigans', heard the couple bickering through the floorboards.

'Are you not able to stand on your feet?' Boomed a deep and spiteful voice. Then followed the sounds of something being dragged.

'Stand on your feet!' It appeared to Mr Quinn that Peter was trying to get his drunken wife to stand up straight, but with limited success. More discordant noises emanated from the Brannigans' room: 'Light the fire or I will throw you downstairs!' Then it sounded as if Mary had been pushed over with considerable force.

Thomas was most worried. He sent his wife Ann out to find a policeman, while he remained to listen. A few moments later Mrs Quinn returned. She could not find a policeman in the vicinity and did not wish to go out any further to search for one alone.

Suddenly the one-sided row ended with the sound of footsteps calmly descending the staircase. From his room, Mr Quinn listened closely as he heard Peter Brannigan send out for some whisky. Brannigan then returned to the top of the house and closed the door.

'Get up and light the fire, we are not short yet!' he growled. 'I have a bottle of whiskey and two bottles of ale. I have bought a hundredweight of coal; I gave you money to buy a lamp but you did not buy one!'

A thud was heard, giving neighbour Thomas Quinn the impression that yet again Mrs Brannigan had been thrown down.

There was silence for about five minutes. It seemed as if the pair had settled down and were quietly drinking, but then all at once there was an exclamation: 'We will have a light on the subject!' Peter announced, before going out into the street and returning a few minutes afterwards clutching a candle. He struck a match and said, 'There's a sixpenny candle. Get up and light the fire!' He also demanded that Margaret come to midnight mass with him.

Directly below, the Quinns were still eavesdropping. They heard rapid footsteps, then an unmistakable and pitiful choking. Peter was throttling his wife. 'Light the fire!' he roared.

Margaret broke free from his grip and gasped for air. 'Oh Peter I cannot!' He called her a foul name before again knocking her to the floor. Until about 4 a.m. the sounds continued as if someone or something was being trailed across the room, at which time Mr and Mrs Quinn went to sleep. However, Thomas' snooze didn't last long. At about 6.30 a.m. he was awoken by yet more noise coming from the room.

'Put on a fire,' Peter grumbled. Margaret only moaned some drunk and unintelligible expression. Her husband complained that he was cold and asked Margaret to cover him. All was quiet. At nine, Thomas was awoken again when Mr Brannigan went downstairs and asked Miss Usher for a cup of tea. He did this a second time shortly afterwards, except in this instance saying, 'I wish there was a fire upstairs. If that poor bitch is not dead she is very near it.'

Shocked, Mary went upstairs with Peter and saw the dreadful state of her friend.

'Oh dear, oh, dear, Margaret, Margaret. I have done it,' sobbed Mr Brannigan, before kneeling down to kiss is wife. 'There is life in her yet!' Dr Kellet Smith was called to the property and made his way up the stairs to the room the Brannigans shared. He found it to be in a most filthy condition and almost devoid of any furniture whatsoever. The floor was littered with coal, old straw and dirty rags. Blood and all manner of unidentifiable liquids seemed to stretch across the whole floor space. The doctor had never seen a more wretched placed in his life.

Amongst this scene of misery lay the naked, dead body of Margaret Brannigan. She was covered by only a small black petticoat, which was wet and covered in grime. On carefully rolling the body over, Dr Smith found only a few strands of soiled straw and clothing, which he could have held in his two hands, to make up what was her mattress. Mrs Brannigan herself seemed well-nourished, yet her body bore numerous marks of abuse: plentiful old scars, various fresh bruises, and two black eyes. The doctor noticed a severe cut above her right eyebrow, from which had evidently drained a great deal of blood. The night had also been extremely cold; this, along with the terrible injuries bestowed upon her by her callous spouse, were no doubt the cause of her death. Syncope, a loss of consciousness, had been brought on and the tremendous shock to her system also played a part in Margaret's passing.

It was heard, however, that the deceased herself was a very drunken woman and when in drink was very violent and was often heard to call her husband awful names which could not be repeated. She would often spend the prisoner's Saturday wages on drink despite the appalling disorder of their rented room.

The jury listened to the facts of the case and after a short consultation found Peter Brannigan guilty of manslaughter. Mr Justice Willis felt it necessary to defer sentencing him until the following day, when he was again brought to court.

'I am satisfied that this misery in which you lived was partly her fault, but I am quite satisfied also that it was partly your fault,' declared the judge. 'The deceased and yourself had the opportunity of living apparently in great comfort for a working man. You were earning good wages as a joiner and you brought part of it home. I am quite satisfied that it was from your own doing that you were reduced to this state of misery and all through your terrible appetite for drink. Yesterday you were in very serious danger of being committed for murder. I certainly think that you had in the jury a favourable tribunal.'

Mr Brannigan was then sentenced to fourteen long years of penal servitude.

REVENGE OF A PIMP

In the year 1862, Thomas Edwards, a butcher, was living at a house in Liverpool's Norman Street. He cohabitated with a woman named Isabella Tonge, and had done so for a number of years. Prior to moving in with Edwards, Miss Tonge had resided with a man called Thomas Sullivan. He had been transported away from Liverpool – and Isabella – for about ten years, but had recently returned to the city after serving out his sentence. He soon tracked down Miss Tonge and took up a room in the same house,

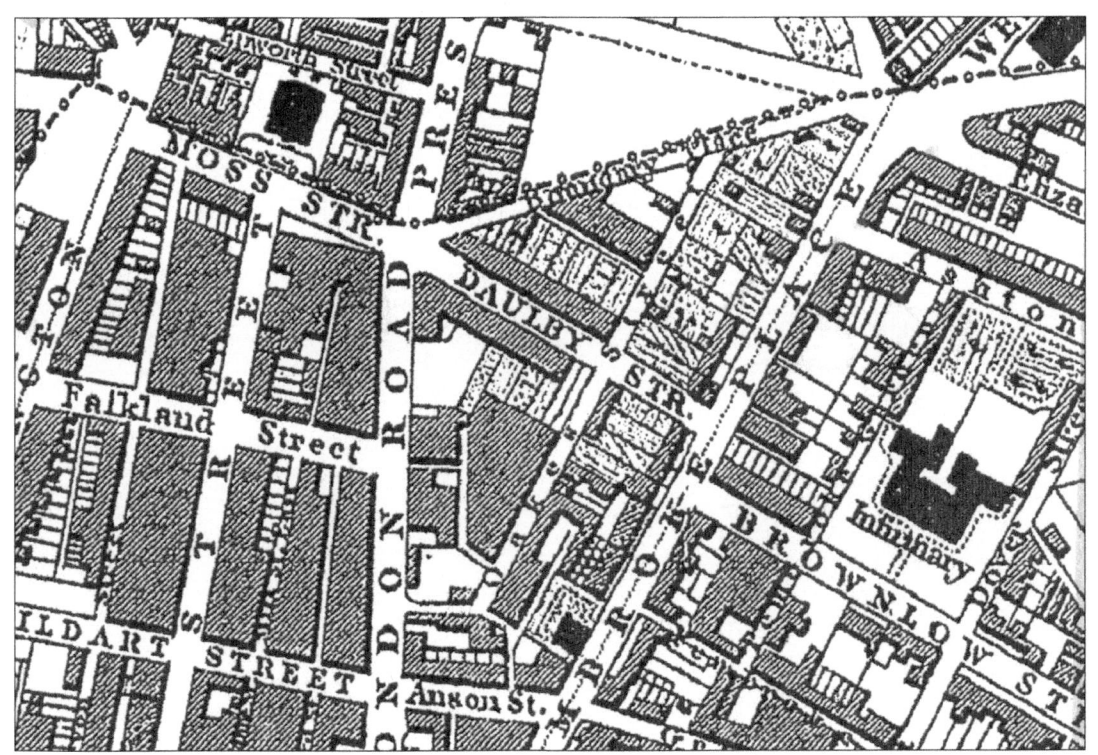

The vicinity of Norman Street, c. 1840.

No. 11 Court, in Norman Street. The intimacy which had previously existed between the two was quietly rekindled, and for several days after Sullivan had arrived back at the house the pair would often disappear together. This caused her current partner, who was left alone at the house, to experience immense rage. It was common knowledge that his girlfriend was a prostitute, but to Thomas Edwards the fact that Isabella had real feelings for this other man proved even harder to swallow.

On 26 November, Sullivan and Tonge left the house at about midday. Consumed with jealousy, the thirty-year-old butcher also left the property to escape the loneliness of Norman Court. He returned at about eight o'clock, when he spoke with Jane Wilson, a fellow tenant at the house. She informed him that Isabella had not yet come back and was still out with Sullivan.

Thomas became most irate and stormed out again to fetch some ale and rum. These he duly mixed together and drank abundantly, drowning his emotional troubles in a sea of cheap alcohol. He eventually fell asleep on the downstairs sofa, only to be awoken at about two o'clock by the sound of the creaky front door. It was them, Thomas Sullivan and Isabella.

'Where have you been the whole day?' Edwards snarled as he began to interrogate the woman who had been his all. Isabella stared blankly and made no reply. 'It does not matter to you where she has been,' said Sullivan, 'she has been out with me.'

Thomas Edwards did not respond but slumped back into the sofa. Sullivan, Isabella and Jane Wilson then took up seats in the room and the group of four sat around the fireplace apparently on friendly terms. After half an hour sitting and chatting, the disheartened tradesman yawned and said that it was time for bed. Miss Tonge declined; she was somewhat apprehensive as Edwards was lazily playing with a knife. Isabella suggested that he and Sullivan should go upstairs and that she and Jane would spend the night downstairs.

Accordingly, Sullivan and Edwards made their way up the staircase, but after a lapse of a few minutes, Edwards returned, in only his shirt and drawers and still carrying the blade. He was now obviously seething and demanded that Jane go to the cellar for some water. 'Now!' he ordered.

Before Miss Wilson had a chance to leave, Thomas began arguing with Isabella and aggressively requested money from her. She refused. 'I shan't prostitute my person anymore for you!' she hissed.

'May God strike me dead. I'll be hung for you yet. You shan't live a week!' fumed Thomas. 'Murder!' cried Isabella. He raised his hand high into the air and brought the knife down, stabbing her repeatedly in her neck and chest.

Norman Street, the scene of the murder of Isabell Tonge.

The screaming woman reached for a pair of tongs from the flickering fireplace and tried desperately to defend herself. The butcher treated her like a piece of meat and continued to slice his way through the raw flesh that was Isabella's body. The woman fell screaming to the floor in a pool of blood. Miss Wilson hurried over to tackle the crazed attacker, only to receive a cut to her hand for her troubles. She fled from the room in search of help and attracted the attention of some passing policemen.

Thomas Sullivan rushed down the stairs and was himself attacked by the madman. He also received several wounds, but of far less severity than those sustained by their common love interest.

More cries filled the house attracting the attention of other residents sleeping within. Catherine Jones, a domestic servant, ran to the bleeding victim and tried to stem the flow. 'You have killed her!' she screamed.

Edwards made no reply but went out into the street half-dressed and covered in gore. He soon returned and went straight up to his room. He dressed himself in normal daywear and headed calmly for the door, seemingly oblivious to the carnage he had just created.

By this time, PCs Micklethwaite and Bell were on the doorstep – just as Thomas was about to make his exit. The officers questioned him about the commotion and told him that they wished to come and investigate.

Thomas grinned; a knife was in his grasp. 'I have been doing my work. If you would like to come inside you will see what I have been doing.' They immediately took the weapon from Mr Edwards' hand. 'That's not the knife I used,' he remarked cheerfully, as the policemen looked on bemused. The two law enforcers cautiously entered the house where they discovered a scene of bloody mayhem. On the sofa sat an awfully dishevelled and anaemic-looking Isabella Tonge. Amazingly, she was still alive, but only just. 'I have had my revenge,' Thomas laughed. 'I wish she would die as I want to be hanged for her.'

Miss Tonge was taken to the Royal Infirmary and was treated by house surgeon Henry Greenwood Rawdon. He did not hold out much hope that his latest patient would recover from her wounds – and indeed, she did not.

The constables arrested Mr Edwards and walked him outside. They escorted him up London Road where they whistled for help in taking the prisoner to the Bridewell. 'Oh you need not whistle for assistance for I'll go quietly with you,' Thomas sniggered. 'You go back to the house and see how she is. See if she is dead. If she is not, I hope she will die, and the man Sullivan also, and I can die with them.'

Later, on being taken from the Prescot Street Bridewell to the Main Bridewell, a fellow officer asked the two men what their prisoner was charged with.

'Stabbing his wife,' replied PC Micklethwaite.

'She is not my wife!' Edwards retorted. 'She ought to have been. We have been asked at church three times, but she got drunk every time and made a fool of me!'

Thomas Crowe, an assistant at Bridewell, asked the accused to pick out which knife he had used from a number taken from the house by the two officers as evidence. 'This is the one with which I did it,' the butcher answered, as he pointed towards a small dressing knife. 'And I hope I did it well as if not I shall finish them.' He was then locked up to await his trial. The following month saw Mr Edwards appear before Mr Justice Blackburn on a charge of wilful murder.

In going through the evidence and summing up, His Lordship directed the jury to question whether the acts of the prisoner which resulted in the death of Isabella Tonge were the consequence of premeditated revenge or the result of her provocation. The number of stab wounds inflicted proved that there was a true intention to occasion some grievous bodily harm and the jury would have to consider that, if there was indeed provocation on behalf of the deceased, whether these injuries could be justified. The judge remarked that due to the quantity of wounds, two of which were mortal, it certainly did appear that the prisoner intended to kill. This, along with the prisoner's repeated comments that he hoped she would die, further suggested to the judge that Thomas was guilty of the charge. The jury retired to consider their verdict and were absent for what seemed an eternity, but was in fact just ninety minutes or thereabouts. Upon their return, a breathless silence prevailed while the clerk of the court asked the jury if they had agreed upon a verdict.

'We have,' answered the foreman, 'we have found the prisoner guilty, but we recommend him mercy.'

'On what grounds?' enquired His Lordship.

After some hesitation the foreman referred to the provocation the deceased had caused with her intimacy with Thomas Sullivan.

The prisoner remained indifferent to the usual inquiry made by Judge Blackburn, asking whether he had anything to he wished to say which may persuade him from passing a sentence of death. Adopting the black cap, the judge uttered the ponderous words: 'You have been found guilty of the crime of wilful murder upon evidence which admits of no alternative. I don't think there was anything upon the evidence which could any way justify the jury in finding a verdict of manslaughter.'

Mr Justice Blackburn was keen to point out that there was no promise that the jury's recommendation of mercy would be brought into effect and that he should place no reliance upon it and savour his last moments of life. Thomas Edwards stood either ignorant or plainly unconcerned regarding the dire straits in which he was placed, showing no remorse until he heard the judge pronounce his sentence:

> It is that you be taken from this place in which you are to the prison from which you came, and from thence on a day appointed to the place of execution, and there be hanged by the neck until the body be dead, and that the body when taken down be buried within the precincts of the prison in which you have been last confined; and may God have mercy on your soul.

Thomas' face turned a wretched shade of white and he suddenly felt sickened like never before. He lost his rebellious demeanour and grasped the front rail in a spasmodic jolt. However, the condemned man soon regained his bravado. Looking around the court, Thomas stared coldly into the eyes of several onlookers, before walking briskly down to the cells to await his end.

On 3 January 1863, Thomas Edwards' wait was over. He was taken to Kirkdale gallows where he was publicly hanged for his vicious and vengeful crime.

A SUSPICIOUS SON-IN-LAW

On the night of Thursday 28 April 1870, James Singleton returned home from a heavy afternoon of drinking. He was in a most intoxicated state and – as usual when he had had a tipple – his mood was one of awful aggression. At about 4.45 p.m. James staggered up to the door of his home, 38 Letitia Street, just off Park Road. He shared the property with his wife and mother-in-law and it was the latter, Mrs Jane Gibson, who would face James's drunken wrath.

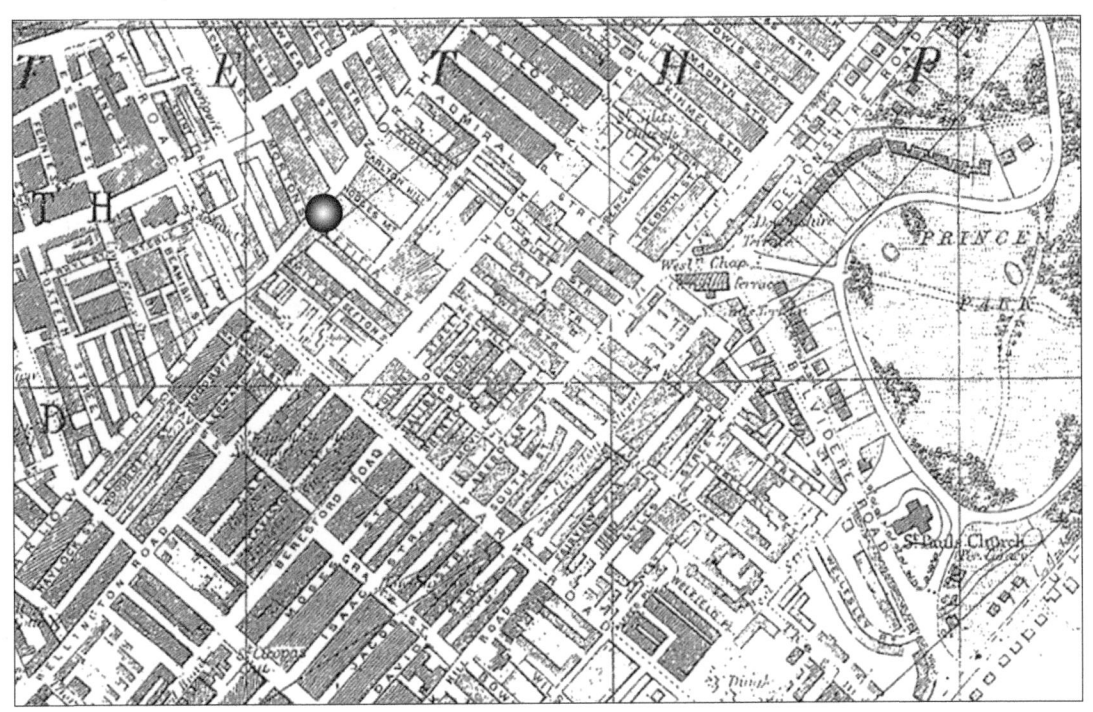

A map of Letitia Street from 1885.

Looking up Letitia Street as it appears today.

For reasons that remain unknown, James launched a fearful attack upon the terrified woman and struck her several times with a ship's scraper. He brought the triangular weapon, made of heavy solid steel and a wooden handle, down hard onto the head of his elderly victim sending flecks of crimson splattering about the room. Ignoring her cries for mercy, Mr Singleton took out a razor and began slicing his mother-in-law's wrinkled flesh open: by the end of this monstrous melee, Mrs Gibson was left bleeding from a number of lacerations to her neck and face, as well as suffering from three fractures of the skull.

He left his victim lying pitifully in a pool of her own blood and headed towards the fields in nearby Warwick Street. It was there that a young boy witnessed the bloodstained spectre throw the blade into a pond. The lad at once went to find a policeman and told him what he had seen. The officer went to the spot described by the youth and found James Singleton covered in blood and obviously drunk. The officer immediately questioned him over the deeply unsettling circumstances that he had found himself in.

'If you go to Hill Street you will know all about it,' hiccupped James. The policeman took James to the street he had mentioned and he pointed out a certain house. The officer knocked on the door and went in. Inside resided Mrs Singleton, James's mother, and she did not have the faintest idea of what her son was talking about. She was under the impression that he had gone to the Sailors Home, but this was not the case.

'He lives with his wife at 38 Letitia Street,' she informed the officer. As the man was drunk and his clothes speckled in blood, the constable told James he would have no choice but to take him to the Brunswick Dock Bridewell. The news did not go down well, and Mr Singleton became very violent and abusive. He refused to accompany the officer and had to be forcibly taken down with the assistance of two further lawmen.

At the station James was booked into a cell for being drunk and riotous. Several officers were then dispatched to the prisoner's house, where they discovered Mrs Gibson clinging on for dear life. Police were told by lodger Alfred Treby that at about 5 p.m. he had heard James Singleton return home under the severe influence of alcohol. Mrs Gibson related as best she could the outrage that was committed upon her and a car was procured for her removal to the Southern Hospital. Doctors ascertained the woman to be in a very dangerous state and police feared that they may soon have a case of murder on their hands.

At about 7 p.m. James, who was still secure in his cell, became incredibly violent, lashing out and screaming as loud as his lungs would allow. Concerned staff believed it necessary to secure the prisoner tight in irons. This was done, but, with seemingly superhuman strength, the psychopath tore the staples from the walls and broke free from his chains. Bridewell keeper Mr Wilson contacted several officers to help him restrain the fearsome inmate once again. A short time later Mr Wilson and the constables entered Singleton's cell, which for several moments had been eerily silent. The men were horrified to discover him lying on the ground with his neckerchief twisted tightly around his throat. James had fastened the end of it to the bottom hinge of the cell door, a mere 2ft or 3ft from the floor. He had then dropped into a reclining position and slowly strangled himself. Medical attendance was immediately sought, but James Singleton's life was already over and extinct.

A CHARRED CONCEALMENT

Late in the evening of 20 September 1895, the officers of E Division received suspicious information regarding a woman living at 68 Leyden Street in Kirkdale. Ann Burke was the wife of a nautical fireman whose husband was away from home. Neighbours of the woman had witnessed a disturbing change in her behaviour of late and noticed how the once relatively normal mother had been acting in a most extraordinary and often

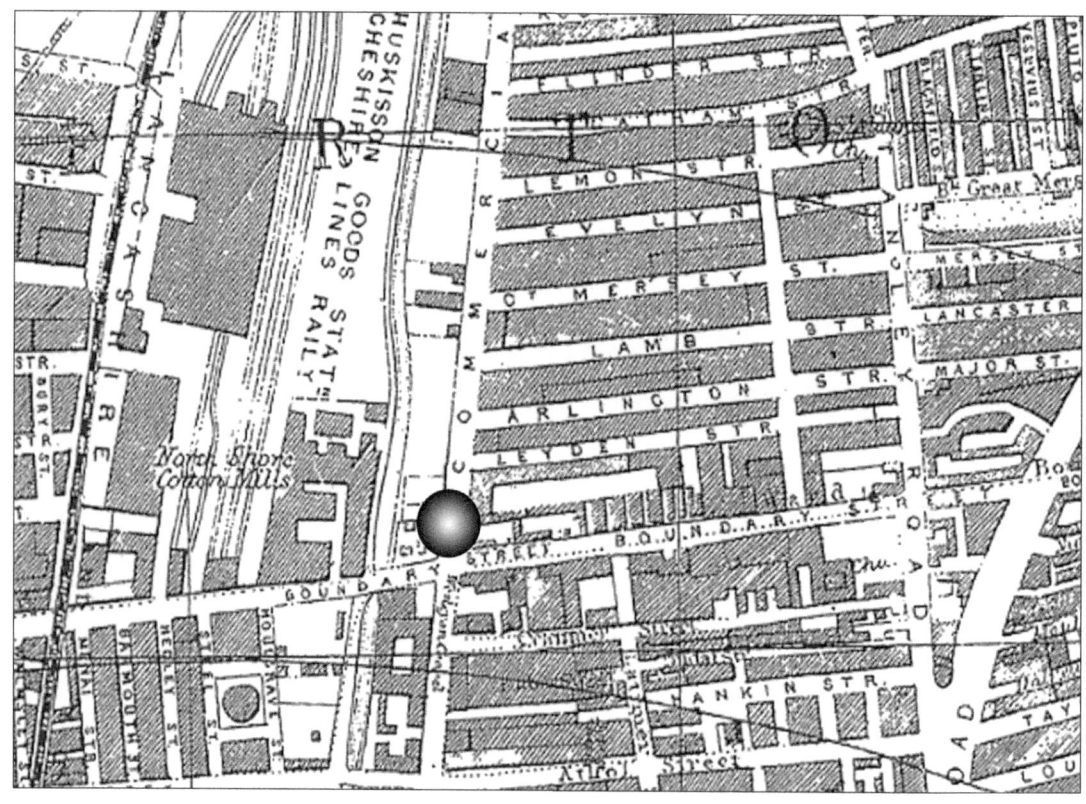

The scene of the baby burning, from a map dating from the late nineteenth century.

The area of Kirkdale where Leyden Street once stood.

intoxicated manner. Worried residents informed police that Mrs Burke's recent eccentricity might cause harm to her young children (who lived with her at the house).

At about nine o'clock Detective Sergeant Bailey, in the company of Detective Inspector Kneale, arrived at the property in Leyden Street and were at once bemused by the scene within. The windows reflected a very strong bright light as if the whole room was ablaze. They hammered hard on the front door and demanded to be let in.

'You cannot come in!' cried Ann. One of the officers left in haste to summon assistance and soon returned with two constables. With the additional manpower the door was charged down, causing a ghastly chill to sweep into the house.

The commotion soon attracted a crowd and a large number of locals gathered outside the property to discover the cause of the disturbance.

Many were anticipating something tragic; many women remarking that Mrs Burke had not been quite right lately. It was heard how a fortnight ago she had been far advanced in pregnancy and had uttered to various neighbours remarks which undoubtedly had aroused some suspicions.

Indoors the sight which was revealed to the officers' was of a most putrid and vile nature. The forty-year-old Ann stood in the middle of the room, a room so unfurnished and bare it was a wonder how the family coped. Her hair had fallen about her neck in a terribly disordered fashion, and her eyes gleamed with a look of pure hate and frenzy. Mrs Burke spat an evil torrent of expletives and insults at the police and wildly attempted to obstruct their entry to the room. This whole terrifying spectacle was witnessed by the woman's eldest daughter. The eight-year-old was crying as she watched her mother's woefully insane performance play out before her frightened eyes.

The roaring fire was thankfully confined to its proper place, but the bright orange flames flew high half way up the blackened chimney breast. From this inferno stemmed the nauseating stench of rotting flesh and within the scorching coals a constable spotted a peculiar outline. He sprang towards it but was scratched and grabbed by Ann who was adamant that the officer should stay back. Mrs Burke was vehemently restrained and the constable headed towards the searing heat to investigate.

The object in the hearth was without doubt the body of a child. The constable bravely reached into the fire and placed his hands around the protruding head – but this proved too hot to handle, and the man recoiled back in pain. He next obtained a nearby poker and shovel and was carefully able to manoeuvre the roasting carcass out onto the floorboards.

The body was that of a newly-born child, charred and burned beyond recognition. The trunk and legs had been almost entirely consumed, but the arms, legs and chest were sufficiently distinguishable to be that of a very young infant. The body was placed in a respectable position before being taken to the detective's office and finally the Prince's Mortuary.

Ann was charged with concealing the birth of a child before being taken to the station.

'I did it. I put it in the fire just before you came in. I must ask you for mercy,' she confessed with a fearful intensity.

The strict examination she was forced to undergo seemed to calm her down, and for the most part told a story of credible coherency. She told police that the child had been born dead and that she had been attended to by a doctor and nurse from Boundary Street. She gave the names of both attendees, but on investigation the nurse and the doctor denied any knowledge of Mrs Burke. Her daughter was questioned but the girl could offer no explanation why her mother was behaving so erratically that evening.

Mrs Burke was taken into custody and charged with the murder of her baby.

'I suppose I shall have to suffer for what I have done,' replied Ann knowingly. Her three remaining children were taken to the shelter to be cared for in Islington.

At the Dale Street Police Court on 20 September, Ann Burke faced Stipendiary Magistrate Mr Stewart charged with the concealment of the birth of her child by secretly disposing of the body. The baby-burner was a fairly tall woman with a pale and drawn face and a mass of messy hair. Her outlandish appearance was completed by a long black cloak in which she was wrapped tight. After serious consideration, Ann was found guilty and sent to the assizes to face the higher court. It was there on 20 November that the prisoner was found not guilty by a learned jury. Mr Connell, on her behalf, successfully argued that the charge of concealment was unfounded. Ann had informed neighbours of her motherly condition and it was well known that she was expecting. There was no way of knowing whether the child was dead when born and without evidence to the contrary, Mr Connell urged the court to find his client innocent. Of course, the manner in which the baby's body was dealt with was deeply unsettling and was an obvious sign that Mrs Burke was of unsound mind. The wise members of the jury consulted and acquitted the prisoner completely, and she was discharged. It is presumed Ann was ordered for psychiatric examination for the sake of her remaining, living children back at 68 Leyden Street.

THE SOLICITOR SHOOTING

In 1908, James Wilcox Alsop headed an eminent firm of solicitors in the centre of Liverpool. Messrs Alsop, Stevens, Crok and Armstrong conducted business from their premises at 14 Castle Street and were well known in the area for their celebrated legal successes. On the afternoon of Thursday 13 February, Mr Alsop was in his first-floor office when the telephone began to ring. He heaved himself up from his paper-ridden desk and made his way across the room to the telephone box. James took a hold of the door and reached forward to pick up the receiver.

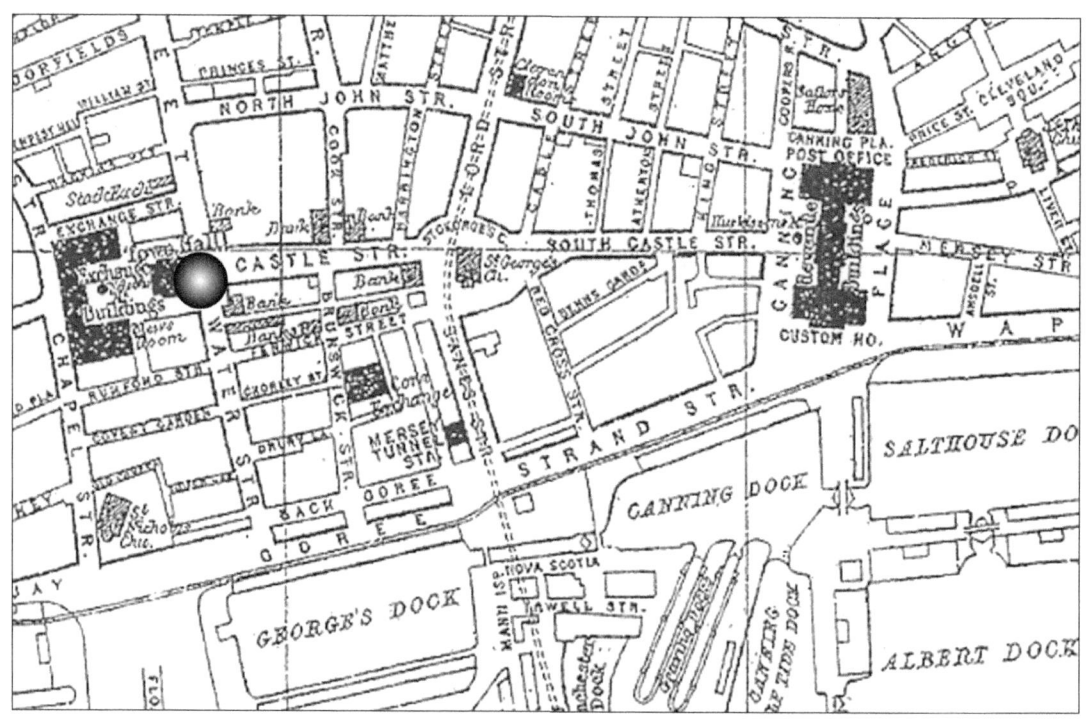

Liverpool's Castle Street, c. 1900.

THE SOLICITOR SHOOTING

The entrance to 14 Castle Street, the building where Mr Alsop was mortally wounded.

Before he could even place it to his mouth, the office door burst open with heart-stopping energy. Mr Alsop barely had time to turn his head before a shot echoed throughout the room. In the doorway stood a crazed gunman. He fired a second time at the solicitor, who by now was clasping his arm in agony. The first bullet had struck his left limb and was now deep inside James's steadily bleeding muscle. The second had missed and was now embedded in the splintered telephone box door. Those in the office wasted no time in chasing the assailant down the stairs and out into Castle Street. The man's wild appearance and careless brandishing of the revolver caused members of the public to run in terror. In Exchange Street East, the running gunman turned and fired towards his pursuers. Luckily the bullet missed, and, shortly afterwards, PC Metcalf courageously knocked the revolver from the madman's grasp and arrested him.

A Victorian look up Castle Street.

Back at the office, Mr Alsop had his arm bandaged and was soon sent to the David Lewis Northern Hospital in Great Howard Street for examination. It was there that Dr Barnes, house surgeon, successfully extracted the bullet and was optimistic of a full recovery. The wound was not serious, but the shock to someone of Mr Alsop's advanced years could have been far worse. After an hour's rest, James was conveyed home to Oxton by the seven-thirty luggage boat to recover.

PC Metcalf had since taken the prisoner to the Dale Street Bridewell. On searching the man, the police found he owned a second revolver. His identity was established as thirty-five-year-old William Stanley Vaughan, of Prescot Street, Liverpool, who until recently resided in Wallasey. William's manner was so strange police sent for the prison surgeon to conduct an examination. He certified that Mr Vaughan was suffering from deranged hallucinations and ordered his removal to the Brownlow Hill workhouse hospital. Vaughn would have been charged with attempted murder under normal circumstances, but he was not currently medically fit to stand trial.

Mr Vaughan made some extraordinary allegations. He told police his father held several farms at Haverfordwest, South Wales; in the previous year the prisoner had alleged in a periodical that he was the rightful owner of the valuable estates of Captain Vaughan, who died in 1875. He also alleged that a solicitor who was found dead in a ditch in Maghull in 1872, his mother, who was found with her throat cut there in 1875, and his father were all murdered. William chillingly related how anyone who had known about the gruesome killings died suddenly themselves, while he laid claim to a fortune of about £1 million.

Furthermore, Mr Vaughan stated that he was brought up in Liverpool and was educated at Preston College. He had lived with his wife in two travelling caravans staying at Magazine Farm in Bromborough before taking up residence in Wallasey. At his current Prescot Street address, he had just opened a small curiosity shop. Despite all these outrageous claims, William did consider himself justified in his attempt to shoot Mr Alsop. The facts were heard before Judge Coleridge at the Liverpool Assizes on 16 May.

Prosecuting for the Crown, Mr Sanderson stated that the prisoner's father had employed Mr Alsop's firm to represent him from 1869 to 1875. Before his death, he executed in favour of his only son, William, a settlement of about £1,000 and all of his property with the exception of a £100 legacy. In 1894, when Mr Vaughan came of age, the property of his father and of another relation of which he was bequeathed was handed over. For some time Mr Alsop's firm acted on behalf of William with regard to certain sales of his new property without any problems whatsoever. It was heard that the last transaction took place in the year 1903, but in 1904 the prisoner began writing letters inquiring about his property and also began involving other solicitors who wrote to Mr Alsop. The firm answered satisfactorily in every way they could, but Mr Vaughan seemed to be fixated on the idea that Mr Alsop was holding papers to which he was entitled to. It was Mr Alsop's view that as solicitors they must hold onto the documents on behalf of the executors, but promised to look into the matter to see if there were in fact any papers that did indeed belong to him. The court listened closely to the intricate details of the case.

It seemed that Mr Vaughan's actions were due to a serious misunderstanding. Mr Sanderson related how on 3 June 1904, the prisoner's patience finally reached its limit. It was on that day that William composed a letter penning what was a furtive death threat, with the sly suggestion that he would go to Mr Alsop's office with the intention of murdering him. From that time until September 1907, James had no more contact with his former client, until one day meeting him by chance in the street.

'What about Treboath Farm?' snarled Mr Vaughan.

'That matter has been explained to your solicitors over and over again,' replied Mr Alsop.

At that William said something to James which he could not now remember, but the words had left a deathly impression in his mind at the time. Mr Madden, for the defence, wished to remind the jury that William Vaughan was not one of the criminal classes, but was well educated and moved in respectable society. Unfortunately his client was a victim of his own delusions, but not so much to call him insane. Rather, his mind was diseased by brooding over trouble, believing he had been swindled out of properties which had been sold and were not of the acreage he thought they were.

'You could reasonably think that Mr Vaughan merely intended to frighten Mr Alsop without hitting him, or to hit a part not vital in order to call attention to his case and get possession of the deeds, or in some way satisfy his brooding mind,' said Mr Madden.

His Lordship remarked that the law only recognised delusions if they prevented a man from knowing he was committing an offence. If the prisoner did not mean to hit Mr Alsop, then why did he fire a second shot?

Mr Madden at this stage of the trial felt compelled to remind His Lordship that there was there was a lesser count against William, one of grievous bodily harm, and if it could be shown that the defendant aimed away from any vital part of Mr Alsop, then the jury had grounds to find a verdict on this charge.

After a few minutes discussing the matter in private, the jury returned to court and announced their decision.

'We find the defendant guilty of wounding with intent to murder,' proclaimed the foreman.

Judge Coleridge wished to deliberate on the sentence until the following Monday. It was then that Mr Sanderson handed His Lordship several letters written by the prisoner to Mr Alsop's bankers, the coroner and to Scotland Yard. He stated that they were not relevant to the trials, and he did not wish to influence His Lordship's decision, but would hope that they would afford his client some direction in regards to the prison authorities.

On passing sentence Judge Coleridge said that Mr Vaughan had been found guilty of wounding with intent to kill.

'My duty as judge is clear. I have to act on the jury's verdict, and the sentence of the court was that Vaughan must be kept to penal servitude for five years.'

William Stanley Vaughan was then led away to suffer his much-deserved period of incarceration.

THE WRONG CLASS

William Mawdsley of Walton was an apprenticed engineer and a contractor on the Lancashire and Yorkshire railway. On 4 September 1880 he arrived at Sandhills station and boarded a train. He entered the second-class compartment as allowed by his ticket and looked for a free seat. There was just one available, and it was opposite Mr Reader, a snobby solicitor's clerk and next to Mrs Campbell. Mrs Campbell removed some packages she had resting to her side, allowing William to take the seat.

'What ticket have you got?' asked Mr Reader aggressively. 'You have no business being in here. Get out. Go to the van!'

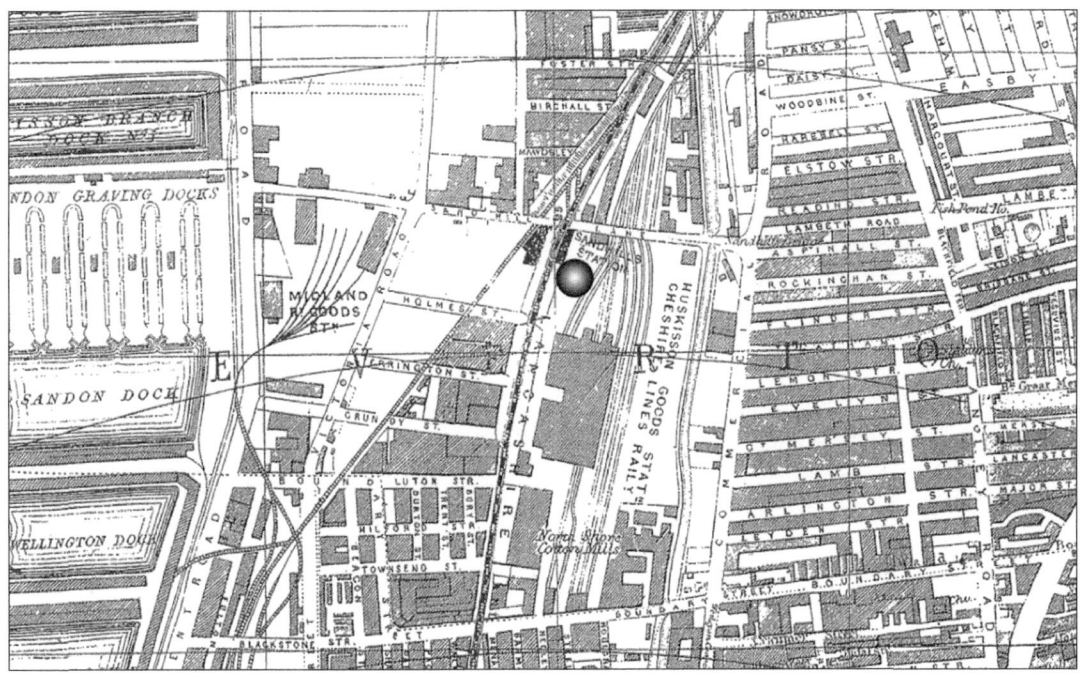

Sandhills station as depicted on this 1885 map.

Sandhills station at the time of its 2008 refurbishment.

'I have as much right to be in here as you do,' answered Mr Mawdsley, his temper quietly raging. He sat back in his seat and folded his arms with a proud smirk.

'You're drunk,' remarked the clerk. 'Guard! Guard!'

'I am most certainly not!' William replied. This hot-blooded exchange continued all the way to Kirkdale where, at the request of the train guard, Mr Mawdsley changed carriages to avoid any more arguments.

'He's definitely drunk,' said Mr Reader as William begrudgingly left the carriage, muttering under his breath.

The case was brought before magistrates two weeks later as Mr Mawdsley pursued a charge of breach of the peace.

In remembering the afternoon's events, William said that he had entered the carriage at Sandhills, dressed in his ordinary work clothes and being perfectly sober. He attested that as soon as he took a seat, the defendant Mr Reader took objection and accused him of being intoxicated. William now asked the clerk to apologise for the totally unfounded allegation, but that was not forthcoming. James Wilson was also travelling on the locomotive that day. He supported Mr Mawdsley's testimony, confirming that he most certainly was not drunk, not even tipsy. He stated that Mr Reader repeatedly accused William of being so, but on what grounds he hadn't the faintest idea. George Dineley said the same. He too was a member of the carriage and witnessed the confrontational events. Mr Norris, the stationmaster at Walton, also told the court that William seemed as sober as a judge and that he had witnessed nothing at all to the contrary.

Mr Madge stepped up for the defence and described the day in question as being extremely hot. Consequently, the complainant stank of grime and grease: his appearance was that of a railway worker and he had all the mechanical odours associated with such an occupation following him around. Mr Madge wished it to be known that his client only accused William of being in drink under stressful provocation and if it would be accepted now, he would like to apologise. In spite of his U turn, Mr Reader wished to call his friend, George Campbell, to the stand.

'I joined Mr Reader at Tithebarn Street station and we travelled together from there in the same carriage, even though I myself am a first class contractor. There were four ladies with us, one being my wife. Both I and Mr Reader expostulated with the complainant for coming into the carriage in the dirty class he was. The young man was excited and impertinent,' said George.

Magistrate Sir Thomas Moss in summing up said that it was improper for the defendant and his friend, Mr Campbell, while travelling in a second-class carriage with a first-class ticket to have issue with a second-class ticket holder coming into the carriage. 'You should rather have gone to the carriage of your own class. Interference with passengers in the manner you displayed would upset all the arrangements of the company.'

Mr Reader was ordered to pay £20 bound to keep the peace for six months and pay all costs.

DEPRESSION OF A CORN DEALER

Fifty-one-year-old George Ramsey Livingstone was a successful corn merchant. He had once been one half of the Messrs Haughton and Livingstone duo, a thriving partnership based in Brunswick Street. Mr Haughton, however, had died some fifteen years previously, leaving George to man the reins of the business single-handedly. Now in his later years, this was proving to be quite a strain and George had spoken to some close friends of his thoughts of retirement. He had always been known as

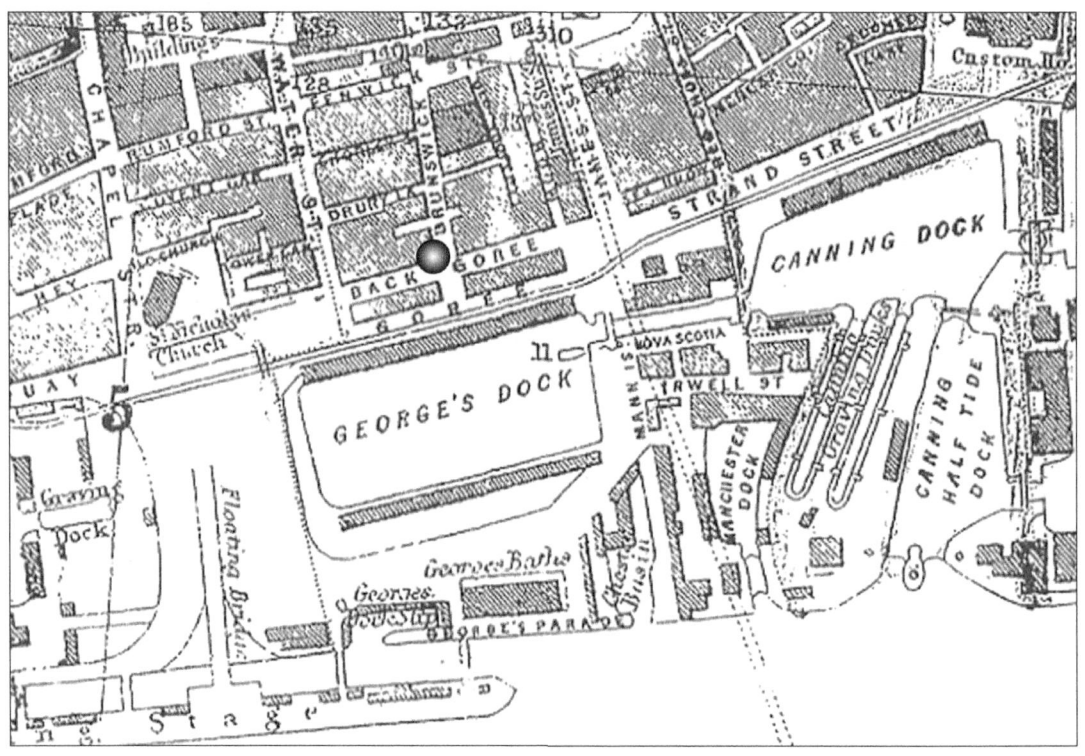

Brunswick Street, as shown in 1891.

Brunswick Street in the year 1923.

a man of integrity and was very much respected by his fellow merchants, his word alone accepted as a bond. Despite his high standing in the corn community, Mr Livingstone was often subject to bouts of depression. It was not unusual for his view to be pessimistic and in recent times this had become morbid to the extreme. Mr Livingstone had not long before been diagnosed with diabetes; six months before, his brother had passed away. On Monday 15 October 1894, Mr Livingstone met with his other brother, the Revd Canon Livingstone, the vicar of Aigburth. It was no surprise that George was in a sorry mood and his sibling tried his best to raise his spirits. 'You cannot understand!' George seethed.

On Thursday the businessman was at his office in Brunswick Street. Edward Kynaston, the manager, was there and George beckoned him to his desk. 'I'll be going to Whitely's to sort out some legal matters,' said George, before standing to put on his coat and hat. The time was about ten to twelve

The view of Brunswick Street, looking towards the river Mersey.

and Mr Livingstone left the building to make the short journey to solicitor's Whitely and Co. Shortly after midday he returned to the office in a somewhat cheery mood and Mr Kynaston left to go on his lunch break.

An hour passed and Edward was feeling quite full. He returned to work and was approached by an office worker. 'Mr Livingstone has been in the lavatory since twenty to one sir,' said the employee nervously. The whole business knew of their boss's disheartened temperament and all expressed grave concern for his health. Mr Kynaston waited some time before deciding to see what the matter was. He headed towards the main office to access the toilet, but this was found to be locked. Confused, Edward acquired a ladder, propped it up against the office door and carefully climbed up. He edged nearer and nearer up towards the partition, feeling more nauseous with every step. Edward peered over and was dumbstruck at the sight which lay before him. Crouched on the floor was the body of George Livingstone in a pool of blood, a revolver at his side. Mr Kynaston jumped down from the ladder and contacted a doctor and the police. Both arrived on the scene quickly but life was already extinct. Officers removed the body with great respect and it was taken away for later interment.

The deepest regret was created in both commercial and social circles at the news of George's death, and at the Corn Exchange the afternoon 'call' was cancelled in respect.

On Friday 19 October an inquest was held into the tragedy by the coroner Mr Sampson. Evidence was given by the office manager Mr Kynaston, the Revd Canon Livingstone, employees Thomas Holloran and William Brown, as well as the testimony of Police Constable Benson, who was the first officer at the scene that fateful afternoon. The jury returned a verdict in accordance with the evidence and declared that Mr Livingstone committed suicide while temporarily deranged. The deceased left a widow, two daughters and two sons.

NUDITY AT LANCELOT'S HEY

In the early hours of 18 July 1869, Police Constable 229 was walking his beat towards Lancelot's Hey, near Chapel Street. In the distance the law enforcer could see a man swaying drunkenly in an open doorway. It was not unusual for the officer to see an intoxicated person at that time in the morning – but the fellow in question was also shockingly naked from the waist down. The constable crossed the street and approached the nude spectacle with caution, before directing the man to go back inside his house, No. 14. The drunk,

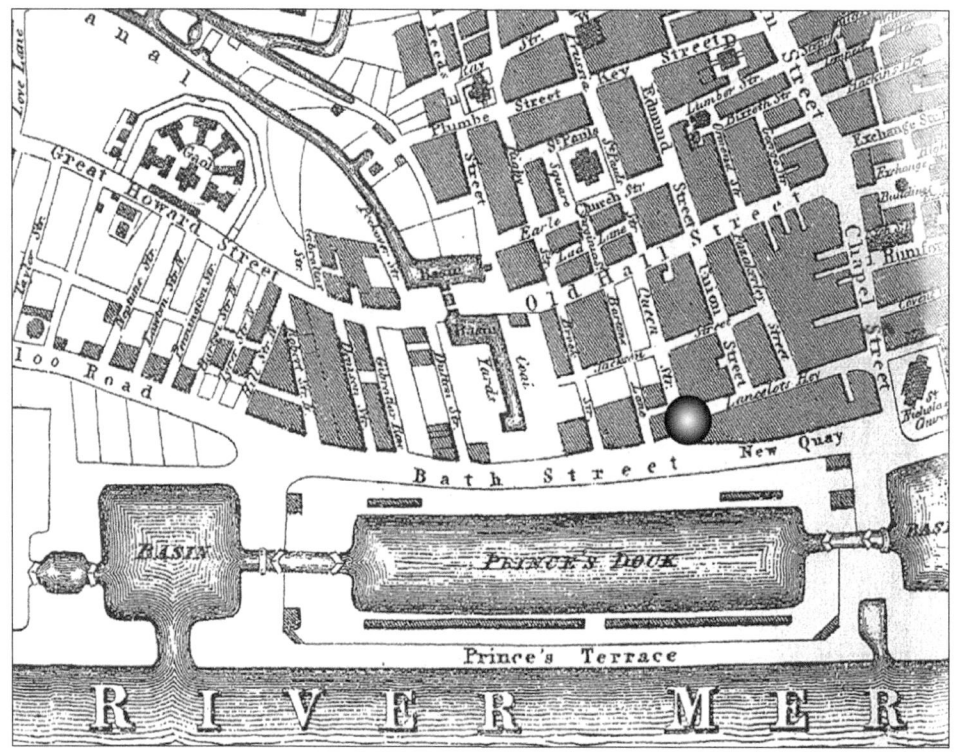

An early map of Lancelot's Hey from 1829.

Robert Lockwood, mumbled an assortment of indecipherable ramblings and expletives, and threatened the constable with a blow to the head. Undeterred, 229 took hold of the drunk and tried to force him back inside.

At this manhandling Robert lashed out and was duly told that he would now have to be taken into custody. At that moment Mrs Lockwood came out on to the front along with their daughter Elizabeth, who was blind. They attempted to prevent the arrest and were warned that if they persisted they too would face a night in the cells. Elizabeth took off her outer skirt and tried to give it to her father in aid of his modesty. She was roughly shoved aside by the constable as he attempted to secure his rather exposed prisoner. The officer whistled for assistance and soon a second bobby was on the scene. 'Please,' pleaded Mrs Lockwood, 'I'll take him home if you will let me.'

The second constable took a more sympathetic view of the situation; the man was half-naked after all, and his poor daughter was disabled. It was no use. Constable 229 was adamant that the girl and her father would be taken to the station and he contacted a third constable. On his arrival a crowd of approximately fifty people had gathered, with angry cries of 'Let her go, she is blind.' The noise awoke Miss Harris who lived next door to the Lockwoods and was a very dear friend to the family. She witnessed the coarse conduct by Constable 229 and went to give him a stern talking to. A few moments into her outburst Miss Harris was grabbed by the officer and told to shut up. All in all he had a grip on Mrs Harris, Robert and Elizabeth. 'You bloody old thing! You ought to be in Rainhill,' he hollered. Witnesses also heard him refer to young Elizabeth as a blind bitch as he struggled to keep hold of the three offenders. A police inspector was contacted and he arranged for Robert Lockwood to be taken away for trial. Mrs Lockwood, Elizabeth and Mrs Harris were told to go home, as was the large and brooding crowd.

On 26 July Robert stood trial at the Dale Street Police Court on a charge of public drunkenness. The beerseller and eating-house keeper stated that on the night in question he had been in bed when he was awoken by the calling of his daughter. Apparently a barrel had burst in the cellar and he was needed to fix it.

'How did you come to be outside?' questioned Magistrate Livingston.

'I was not outside,' answered Mr Lockwood, despite numerous accounts contrary to his reply.

Elizabeth Lockwood was helped to the stand. She deposed that on the night of the 12th a barrel had burst in the cellar and that she had called for her father to go and take a look at it. Having seen to the barrel, the girl

Typical Victorian houses in Lancelot's Hey.

said that Robert went towards the front door where he was at once called by a policeman. She heard her father jokingly ask if the officer was English, Irish or Scottish. To her it seemed that the PC was having none of it and she attested that the man soon assaulted her father quite seriously, and dragged him down the street. She said that she followed and took off her top skirt to hide his nudity. 'That's when the officer struck me,' added the girl.

A neighbour alleged that he saw Mr Lockwood be taken down the street in nothing but his shirt. 'I had never seen a man more abused in my life.'

The police inspector said that he had never had any trouble from the Lockwood household in the past, and they had lived there for a good twenty-five years. He told the court that he had been on the scene that morning and spoke to Police Constable 229. He was not drunk, as some people in the crowd had suggested.

Mr Livingston said that he thought the officer should have issued a summons in the first instance of trouble, rather than carry on with the preposterous charade that had unravelled. Evidence however was satisfactory to prove that Robert Lockwood was not sober and therefore a fine of 5s was imposed. Nothing more was said of the alleged brutality of Police Constable 229.

MISTRANSCRIPTIONS

In September 1848, registration inspectors were perplexed to find a number of unusually similar entries in the birth books for the Great Howard Street sub-district of Liverpool. Things didn't add up, and after close examination by officials, registrar Charles Chubb was arrested. He was charged with obtaining commission under false pretences from the parish officers and brought before Mr Rushton to stand trial.

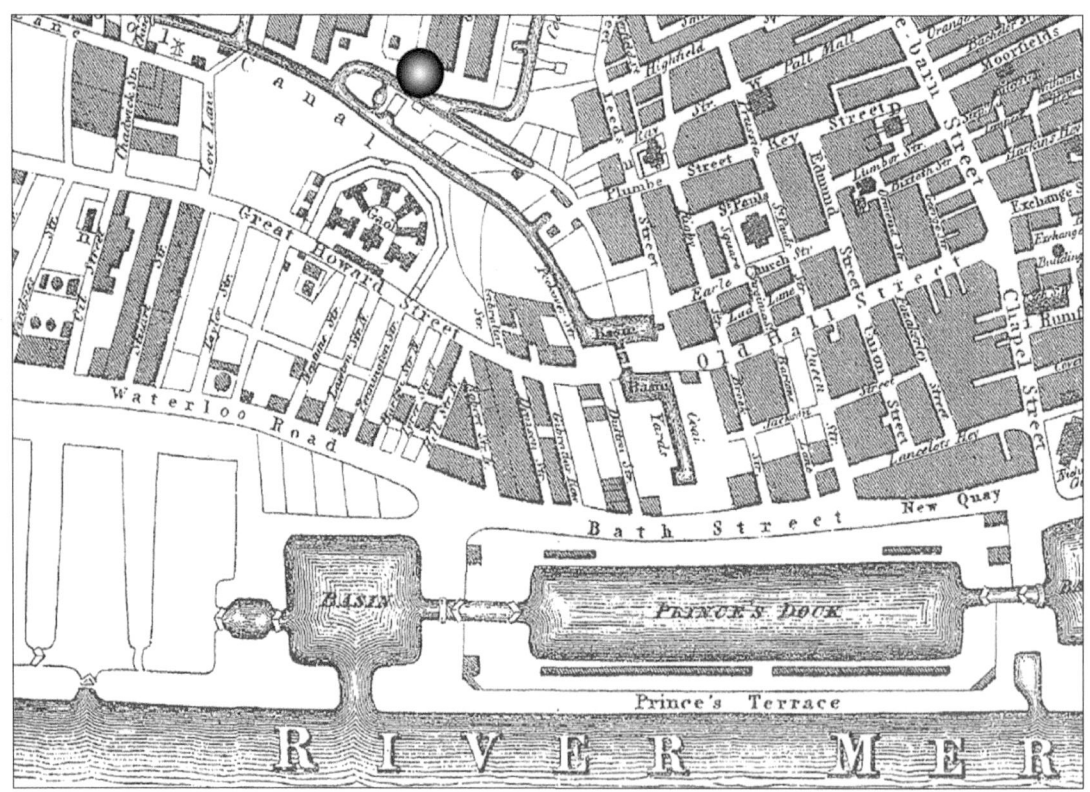

Eaton Street, just off Vauxhall Road, as shown in the early nineteenth century.

Eaton Street, the residence of witness Eliza McKenna.

Seven examples of Mr Chubbs' alleged fake handiwork were shown to the court. All had been registered on 22 August of that year and five of the entries bore an uncanny resemblance to each other. It was clear that a certain curvature to the letters were virtually identical, suggesting that each had been written by the same individual.

A number of witnesses were called and testified against Charles Chubb. Eliza McKenna, of Moss Court, Eaton Street, stated that she had given birth on 21 July. Eliza said that she had visited the registrars' office and informed Mr Chubb of the details. Her son James, however, had been mistranscribed as Patrick, and the father's name as Thomas, when it too should have been James. The book was shown to the court and it was plainly visible that a mark, a small black cross, had been left by Mrs McKenna confirming the details.

'But I never signed the book,' asserted Eliza. If this was true, Mr Chubb had falsified her mark and therefore committed a forgery.

Magistrates sent the accused to stand trial before Sir William Erie, Justice of the Queen's Bench. He was this time charged under the General Registration Act, that he being registrar of births and deaths for Great Howard Street district did feloniously make a false entry of the birth of Mary, the daughter of Ellen Bibby, of 4 Eaton Street, knowing such entry to be false. There were also several other indictments against him for similar offences.

The prosecution outlined how Mr Chubb should have carried out his work, before beginning their verbal attack on the clerk and his illegal misdemeanours:

> The prisoner was the registrar of the Great Howard-street district. He filled the office for some time and had discharged his duty properly, but it was afterwards discovered that the population in that district increased in a very extraordinary manner, for the entries were much greater than could possibly occur in any fair register. This led to an inquiry, and it was found that the book contained a number of entries of births which had not taken place.

As the critical truth began to leak out, it quickly became obvious that Mr Chubb was in all probability a blatant fraud. Mary Bibby didn't even exist, and no such person as her supposed mother Ellen Bibby had ever lived in Eaton Street. The entry in the document was fictional, as was the set of other entries which, as Charles still protested, were in fact genuine.

Charles's assistant, John Eckersley, was asked to stand and testify. He described how on 8 September he had paid a visit to the prisoner and requested the birth register. John said he was given the large italicised book and scanned the notes. Seven entries were added the previous month on the day of the seventh, one being that of Mary Bibby. That addition and the six others were all seemingly written in Chubb's own handwriting with all having only a seemingly innocent mark of an X, but no signature.

Pressed by the prosecution, John admitted that sometimes he had been ordered to have new mothers only sign a blank register book, taking down their particulars on a separate 'waste book' to be added later by Charles Chubb.

The identity of Mrs Bibby was proving somewhat difficult to ascertain. James Jones told the court that he had lived at 4 Eaton Street and had never known any such woman in all his life. The same was said by Mary McCrudden who lived in the cellar under Mr Jones.

Charles employed another assistant by the name of John Hughes. He entered the witness box and told the court that he was an experienced clerk paid on commission of 1*d* per entry. Usually he would have the main book signed by new parents and take down their particulars roughly in the waste book to be added to the register later. John mentioned that if the client could not sign their name, he himself would put a little cross in his waste book to say so. By doing this he knew that on 22 August he had not taken the register anywhere as there were no corresponding notes in the waste book.

Mr Hughes confessed that he had frequently told Mr Chubb of errors and false information but no one had followed it up. Under cross-examination it was revealed that the witness had once been employed by a Dr Walton, working on a commission basis of 4*d* per child he vaccinated. During his time with the doctor he was accused of claiming more than his work's worth, but the case had been discharged by Magistrate Rushton.

Charles' attorney Mr Wilkins made one last plea for the jury to find his client innocent:

> No doubt several false entries have been made, and presuming the jury should acquit the prisoner of the felony, he must leave the court subject to the charge of negligence and irregularity. In the first instance Mr Chubb was in the habit of sending round an assistant to collect as much information as possible. Mr John Hughes was so employed by Mr Chubb and after a time he unwisely believed that he could entirely repose confidence in Hughes and allowed him to take the register book. Mr Hughes obtained the information and entered it in a waste book, but had the informant sign in a blank register and Mr Chubb filled in information from the waste book and put his name to them, believing implicitly every one of them to be correct. Mr Chubb was in receipt of between £300 and £400 a year by his wife and the same amount was settled on him by his father.

'Was it therefore likely,' continued Mr Wilkins, 'that a man in his position, for the paltry consideration of a few shillings would run the risk of confiscating the whole of his property and rendering his wife and children the wife and children of a convict father?'

The jury thought so, and after a short summing up by Judge Erie passed sentence. 'Charles Chubb, you stand convicted of the crime of making a false and counterfeit register of a birth which it was your duty to have kept true. Yours is an offence which in its consequence is likely to produce the greatest possible inconvenience to society.' He was then imprisoned with hard labour for six months.

A DAY AT THE DENTIST

A rather sad and unfortunate case was heard at the Coroner's Court on Wednesday 14 November 1894. That afternoon Mr Sampson and a jury heard the awful particulars surrounding the demise of thirty-seven-year-old Ada Lancaster.

The previous week Mrs Lancaster received a letter from Mr E. Osborn, a Rodney Street dentist, requesting that she did not eat any food before coming

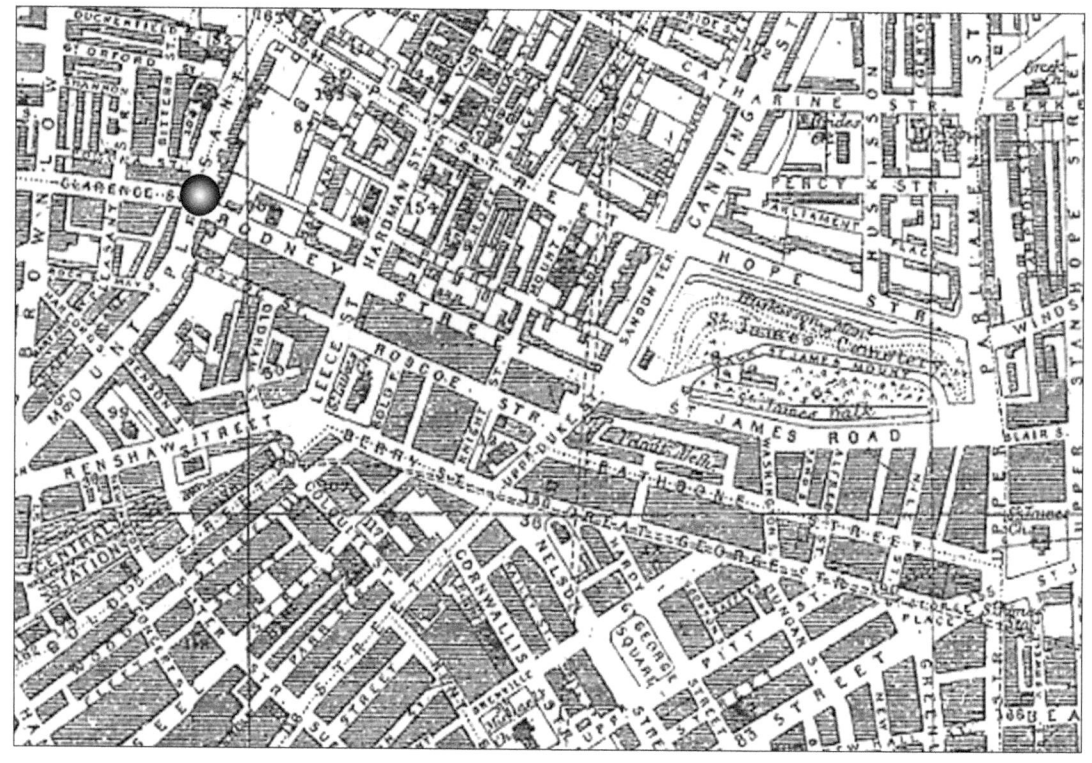

Rodney Street from map dating from the turn of the 1900s.

The former dentist practice in Rodney Street.

to see him for a procedure that was scheduled to be carried out on the 12th. Ada had been a patient at his practice for years and was always confident in Mr Osborn's ability as a dental surgeon.

She headed to his surgery, Osborne, Lewis & James, at 1 Rodney Street and waited to be called. Shortly afterwards Mrs Lancaster found herself in the formidable dentist's chair and was soon being prepared for the procedure. Dr Larkin was to deal with the precarious business of anaesthetisation and began asking the standard questions to determine the woman's suitability for the anaesthetic. Everything was fine.

Mr Osborne retrieved a dental mask from a cabinet and handed it to the doctor. He placed it over the patient's mouth and nose before administering some chloroform. This caused a sweet-smelling aroma to issue up through Mrs Lancaster's throat and nostrils and she began to feel sleepy. Several years ago Ada had undergone a similar procedure with no problems, but this time things were not to go so well. There was a slight struggle before drifting into unconsciousness, but Ada's body seemed to calm down without causing the dentists any cause for concern. It was only when Mr Osborn positioned himself over the woman that they noticed a problem. Her skin had turned a ghostly shade of white, and Dr Larkin could detect no trace of a heartbeat.

Mrs Lancaster, however, did appear to be breathing. Mr Osborne called for his son and Dr Briggs from the house next door who both rushed in to administer any assistance that they could. For two hours artificial respiration was kept up, but to no effect. Mrs Lancaster was dead.

The authorities were contacted and Ada's body was taken away to undergo a post-mortem. Dr Chapman, the physician at the Mill Road Infirmary, conducted the examination. He found the deceased's body to be in a very good condition, the only complaint being that of the early stages of kidney disease. All the organs were in good health and the heart especially was fine in every respect. It appeared to have just suddenly ceased to beat and never resumed.

The coroner asked Dr Chapman if he could account for its sudden stoppage. 'I cannot,' said the doctor. 'It seems one of those lamentable cases, happily very rare, which occur under chloroform. The kidney disease did not in the least affect the case.'

Dr Larkin, the professional who had induced Mrs Lancaster's unconsciousness, was heard to have had twenty-seven years' experience with anaesthetic and had dealt with over 3,000 cases with chloroform. The jury returned a verdict of death from misadventure and stated that it was their opinion that everything possible had been done by the doctors and that the chloroform had been skilfully administered.

MYSTERIOUS CIRCUMSTANCES

The penultimate year of the nineteenth century saw widower Agnes Watts living at the Maid's Home in Charter Street, Manchester. Since her husband's death the thirty-one-year-old had fallen on hard times and was a noticeable character due to the fact she possessed only one eye. Also at the house resided Annie Smith, a woman of similar age who was very quiet and kept herself to herself. She never mentioned anything personal and when asked about her family, she used to cry.

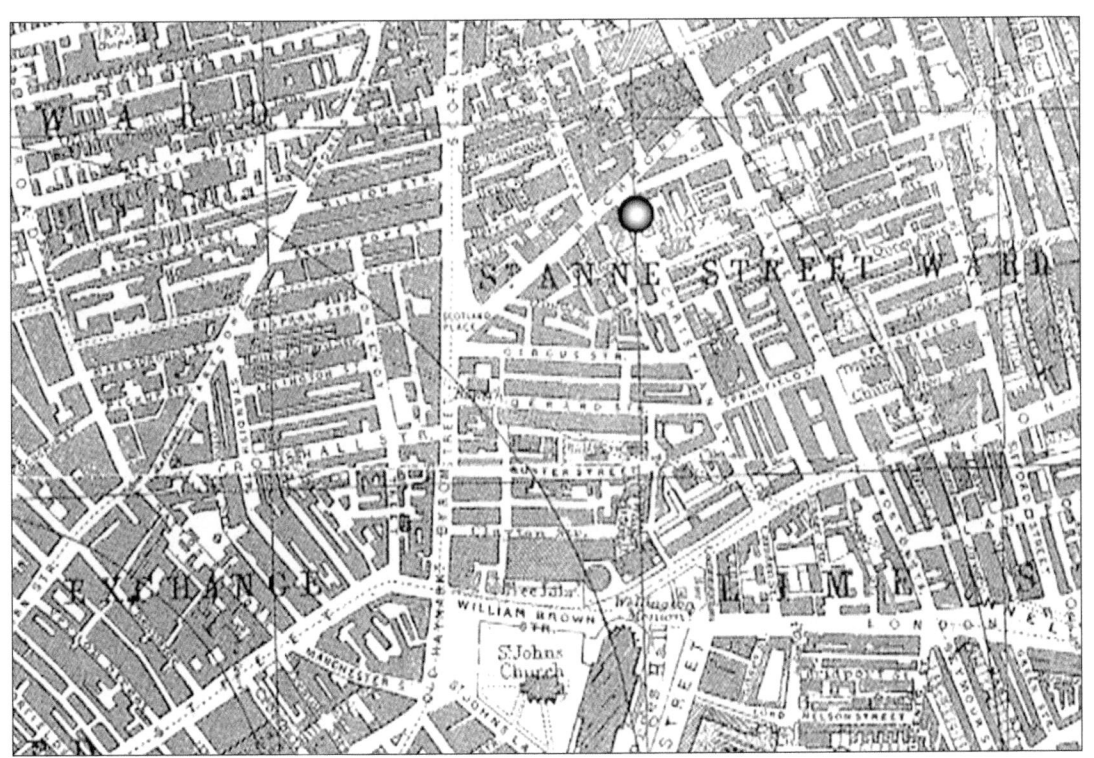

The vicinity of Christian Street and Springfield Place, as shown in 1891.

A week before Christmas Miss Smith had informed Agnes that she would soon be leaving to find accommodation at a place called Lampoil Jack's, which she had heard of in Deansgate. Widow Watts said her goodbyes and believed that would be the last she would ever see of Annie Smith.

On 6 January, however, Agnes came to Liverpool. She walked the distance in stages and was no doubt exhausted on finally reaching the city. The woman neared Park Road, near to St Patrick's Chapel, where, to her astonishment, she saw her old acquaintance from the Maid's Home. She watched as Annie sang somewhat woefully on the street corner. This was how she made her living. Mrs Watts thought it best not interrupt the performance and carried on with her business. She had no idea how long Annie had been in Liverpool, but presumed that Deansgate hadn't worked out for her.

On the afternoon on the 11th, Sarah Evans of Christian Street needed to speak with her sister-in-law. Sarah set off in search of her relative, but her hunt was cut short when she stumbled across a shocking scene: on looking through the window of 18 Springfield Place, the labourer's wife observed the naked body of a woman lying cold upon the floorboards. She screamed for the police and grabbed hold of Constable Gavin to inform him of the news. The officer entered the property and knelt over the body. The unclothed cadaver was very thin, emaciated and covered in dirt and vermin. The eyes seemed sunken but there were no serious marks on the face or head. The constable did notice that the right arm and right side of the body were covered in scars, practically for the whole length of her height. The left arm just below the shoulder was blackened and discoloured, but there did not appear to be any obvious cause of death.

News of the discovery spread quickly and it was not long before Widow Watts contacted the police. She had heard a rumour that a female street singer had been found dead and wondered if it was her old friend, Annie Smith. Police escorted the woman to the Princes Dock Mortuary and showed her the body. She identified it as being so.

In Dale Street on Monday 16 January, the coroner Mr Sampson opened an inquest into the grisly circumstances. Since the discovery Detective Sergeant Duckworth had travelled to Manchester to make enquiries with Mrs Watts. They had been unsuccessful in their attempts to locate further details surrounding Annie Smith. None of her friends or family could be found, forcing them to return to Liverpool and report to the inquest none the wiser. Detective Sergeant Duckworth did however provide information regarding the house in Christian Street. The door, he described, only needed

The remaining portion of Springfield Place.

a little pressure to open it, and the house could be entered easily by a number of other methods. The property had been occupied by vagrants for about four months as a place to sleep, but the officer had no recollection of seeing the deceased in the neighbourhood.

Dr Cornett had made a post-mortem but had found nothing that would lead him to confirm a precise cause of death. The only injuries he found were to the woman's right side. It was covered in scars, just as Constable Gavin observed upon finding the body. 'They could have been caused by her dragging herself across the floor, or from a fall,' said the physician. It was his opinion that the woman had died from starvation and exposure, and due to her emancipated condition death may have been accelerated because of these injuries. The female's nakedness may well have been to escape the itching of the vermin that were found to have plagued her body.

Horace Dunnett, also of Spring Place, related how on the 2nd of that month he had heard cries of 'Help!', 'Murder!' and 'Police!' coming from an empty house there. He stated that the cries were not repeated but it sounded as if someone was being beaten. Such sounds were common in the neighbourhood so little notice was ever taken of them; drunken women were often thrashed by their husbands.

Shortly afterwards the coroner declared that the case had been looked through enough, and wished the jury to consider a verdict. After a brief consultation the foreman stood and announced their collective view: 'Death of woman unknown, supposed to be Annie Smith, death was caused by starvation and exposure, accelerated by injury. How the injuries were received, there is no evidence to show.'

THE BULLY

Michael Lavelle was a sawyer's assistant employed at a timber yard in Bryom Street. On the afternoon of 1 February 1886, he entered the yard and spoke with another worker, forty-two-year-old Maxwell Kirkpatrick.

'How are you getting on?' asked the youth, and an unusually polite conversation occurred between the two. 'When did you start? I should have started a week ago,' said Michael. Mr Kirkpatrick was busy and really didn't

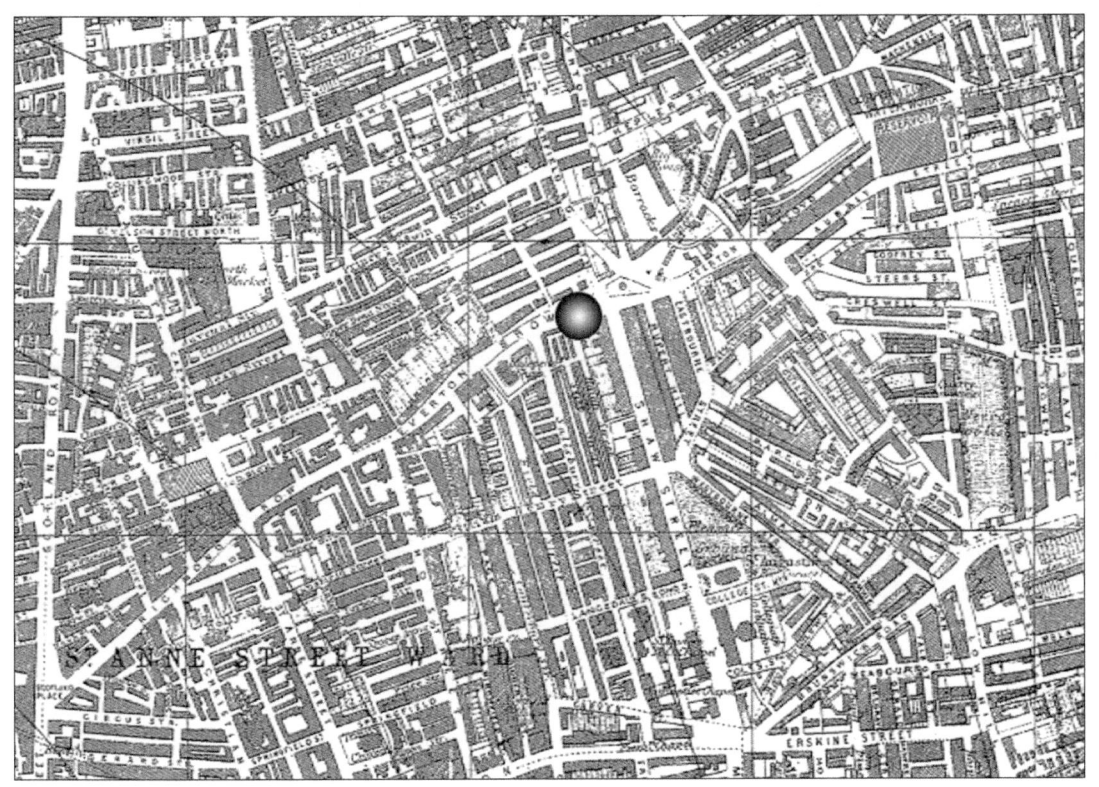

An 1885 map of Everton Brow where Maxwell Kirkpatrick was fatally struck.

A twenty-first century view down Everton Brow.

have time for this idle chit-chat. He quickly brought an end to the talk and got back to his work. Michael decided to go over and look at a boiler and childishly began playing with the steam whistle. 'Leave it alone!' Max shouted angrily. 'It's in the fitter's hands!' The sixteen-year-old left his industrial toy and struck up another conversation with the man. The words exchanged this time were not overheard, but to fellow sawyer's assistant William Roberts, they didn't look pleasant. Michael was irate. He walked away from Mr Kirkpatrick and spoke to William instead.

'Will you be walking home with him?' seethed Lavelle. 'Up Richmond Row or Clayton Street?'

'Yes I'll be going home with Maxwell. I walk past his house on my way,' replied William. 'Richmond Row will be the nearest route,' he added. 'Good night then,' Michael said cheerfully before turning to walk off home. Just then William called to him. 'Do you live in Addison Street?'

'No, no, I'm in Sawney Pope Street,' answered Lavelle. The time was just after 5 p.m. and the workers at the timber yard were preparing to head off for the day. William jogged over to Mr Kirkpatrick and the two left the yard together and headed out towards Richmond Row. Soon they found themselves near to the Congregational Chapel in Everton Brow and it was there that Roberts heard a voice shout out from behind. 'Hello Max!' was the cry. William turned fast, but he was too late to prevent his companion from being struck by an assailant and falling to the ground. It was Michael Lavelle, and in his hands he held a bloodied roller from the timber yard. He had attacked Mr Kirkpatrick and was fleeing the scene via Watmough Street.

'Mr Kirkpatrick? Mr Kirkpatrick?' There was no answer. Maxwell had been knocked unconscious by the blow, leaving the youth Roberts bemused at what to do. Fortunately, his worry was short lived as the sawyer came to in about five minutes.

'What happened?' he moaned. Roberts informed him of the attack, saying that it was definitely Michael Lavelle who was responsible. With the boy's assistance Maxwell was able to walk home. He had blood oozing from his right ear.

After reaching home at about 5.45 p.m., Mr Kirkpatrick spoke with his wife, Jane. 'Is there any blood on my head?' he asked her.

'No dear, but there is some on your ear and neck,' she answered, with a clear tone of concern. She told him he was to see the doctor at once and urged him to see Dr Ellis over at Brougham Terrace. Upon examination the doctor told Maxwell to go home and get some rest. He would be paying a visit later that evening to check up on him and the progress of the injury. Dr Ellis arrived as promised but was met with a hysterical Jane Kirkpatrick, who informed him that her husband had slipped into unconsciousness. Despite the doctor's greatest efforts and an all-night vigil, Maxwell did not regain consciousness and died at 10 a.m. the following morning.

The police were contacted and Detective Sergeant MacDonald and Sub Inspector Hale were assigned to the case. They visited 49 Addison Street that very morning and entered the teenager's bedroom. 'Get out of bed and put some clothes on!' ordered the officers.

'What for?' groaned Michael, still half asleep. 'For seriously assaulting Mr Kirkpatrick in Everton Brow last night!' replied Detective Sergeant MacDonald.

The boy began to cry. 'I used to work with him at Tickle's timber yard and he was always getting on at me,' he whimpered. 'He told me that my mother

Everton Brow. The stone structure, Prince Rupert's Tower, was built in 1787 and used to incarcerate criminals until they could be tried.

was in hell, and I had it in for him for that. I struck him on the top of the head with a stick and then ran along Watmough Street.'

The juvenile's tears failed to elicit any sympathy and at one o'clock, Michael Lavelle was formally charged with causing the death of Maxwell Kirkpatrick. 'I know I did the deed!' Michael cried, 'I want some witnesses!'

Further information from the prisoner yielded the discovery of the murder weapon located in the cellar of a house in Bute Street.

On Wednesday 3 February, the accused attended the inquest into the death before Mr Clarke Aspinall.

Seventeen-year-old William Roberts deposed that he lived at 36 Kepler Road and that he had worked at the timber yard with the prisoner and the deceased. Under cross-examination William said that Michael was 'puller off' for Mr Kirkpatrick at Tickle's yard where they all used to work. During his time there he saw Maxwell constantly bully and demean the lad. It was heard how on one occasion, the deceased had been winding Michael up by throwing chips at him and using abusive language. Master Lavelle lost his temper and threw a roller at the man's legs.

Teenager John Brown was also called to give evidence:

> I worked at Messrs. Tickle and Son's timber yard with Michael and Mr Kirkpatrick. I left about a month ago and the week before leaving I saw Kirkpatrick throw some chips at Lavelle, and heard him call the same an Irish pig. Michael threw a roller at him in return. The same night in the yard, Lavelle said to me, 'I'll be hung for him if he does not leave me alone' and also said that Kirkpatrick's time would be short.

William Tickle, timber merchant of Blackstock Street, was called on behalf of the accused juvenile. He said that the boy had been in his employ for about two months and bore a good character. When Kirkpatrick was employed there were frequent complaints of bullying and it was reported that the sawyer had been ill-using the lads. Hugh Wilson, foreman to the previous witness, backed up the reports of bullying by Maxwell and remarked that the boy was a quiet and inoffensive chap who lived in constant fear of the dead man.

Dr Ellis was next to take to the stand. He had made a post-mortem examination upon the body of Maxwell and found the cause of death to be compression of the brain due to haemorrhage from fracture of the skull.

The jury after some consideration returned a verdict of wilful murder and the prisoner was accordingly committed to the assizes.

At the Liverpool Assizes before Mr Justice Day, Michael Lavelle stood with a capital charge hanging over his youthful head. The accounts heard at the coroner's court were reiterated with one new piece of evidence being mentioned. Michael attested that his and Mr Kirkpatrick's ill-feeling started back in June. According to him, the deceased hit him and grabbed him by the muffles, almost choking him. Two weeks before Christmas Max got his money and went with Lavelle for a noggin of whiskey.

'Once he had the whiskey in him he was like a madman. He kicked and thumped me for nothing!' Michael pleaded.

Dr Commins, addressing the jury for the defence, said that the case was a very miserable one from beginning to end, the deceased appearing to have played the part of a bully and a coward.

'The prisoner was no doubt exasperated by all of his ill-treatment, but no one could have supposed that with such a weapon in the hands of such a feeble lad like him, a blow inflicted upon a strong, powerful man like Mr Kirkpatrick would have had such terrible consequences.' Dr Commins added that there was nothing in the evidence which would lead the jury to suppose that the prisoner had murderous intent. He therefore implored them to consider his client to be only guilty of manslaughter.

His Lordship in summing up said that it was very painful to see a lad of the prisoner's age and who had previously born an excellent character considering the position he occupied. 'However I am here to administer the law without reference to persons. I have to assume that persons intend the natural consequences of their acts and if the consequence of their actions were death, then the person by whom it was committed was guilty of murder.' Judge Day continued by saying that if the jury believed Michael Lavelle intended to commit grievous bodily harm, then he was now guilty of wilful murder and it would be their duty, however painful, to bring in a verdict in accordance with the law.

Half an hour passed before the jury returned from their consultation room armed with a verdict of wilful murder.

'I did not intend to kill the man!' cried out Michael, whose quiet sobbing came to its tender climax.

'With a strong recommendation for mercy,' concluded the foreman. His Lordship sighed. He reached for the black cap and placed it on his head. Lavelle was then addressed:

> Michael Lavelle, you have been found guilty of wilful murder on evidence which is overwhelming against you. You did maliciously kill the unfortunate man, whom you hurried out of his life without one moment of time to repent of the sins he may have been guilty of. Do not fail to at once prepare yourself for the great change which awaits you.

The boy was then led away.

A FIERY FELINE

On 22 October 1896 Sarah Dawber was busy in the back yard of her home having finally found some time to deal with a few household chores. Much to her surprise, a ghastly screech broke the afternoon calmness and a flickering feline flew into full view. A scrawny cat, one Sarah had seen on a number of occasions strutting casually about the cobbles, seemed a lot

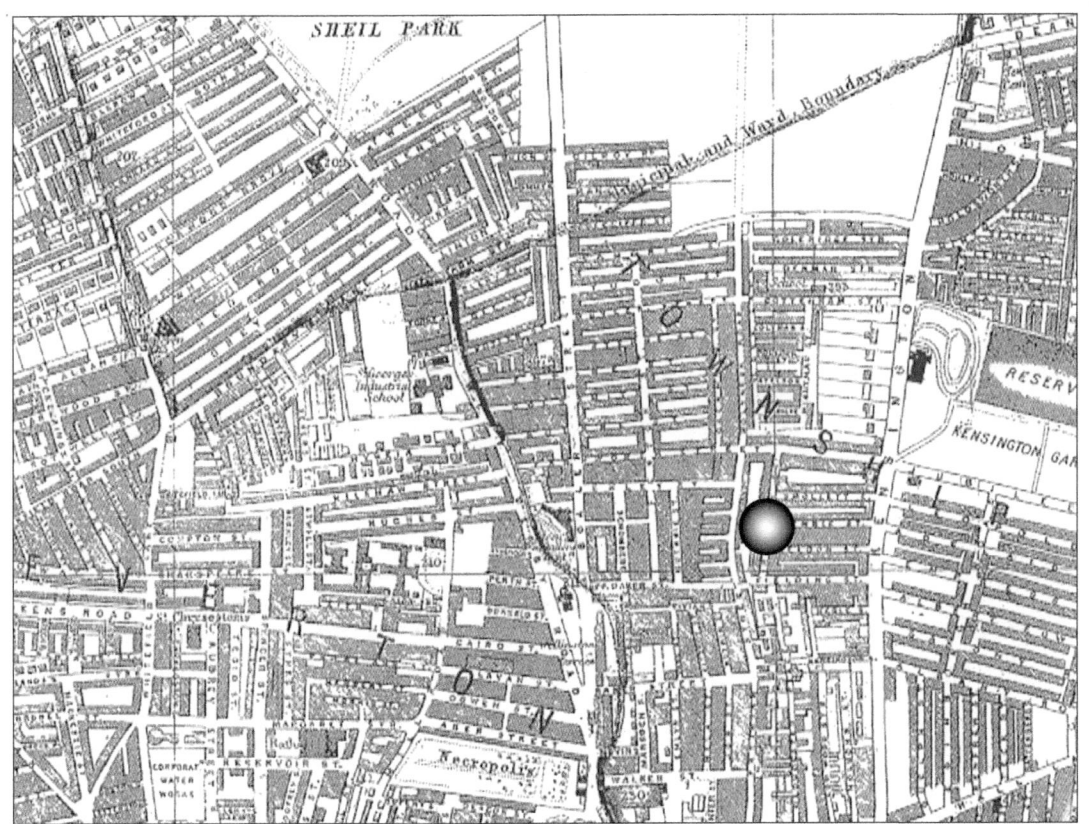

Kemble Street in 1891.

A recent vista of Kemble Street.

more heated than usual – it was on fire! It ran past Mrs Dawber and through her kitchen door. She chased it and tried to shoo the cat back out to the less flammable back yard. The flames of its fur were reaching heights of about 2ft and the kitchen was in serious danger of catching alight as well. Mrs Dawber filled a bowl of water and poured it on the puss, but it did nothing but make the cat cry out louder. It fled through the living room and out the front door to die a slow, hot death.

Inspector Osborn of the RSPCA was contacted and he examined the smouldering carcass. The cat was terribly burnt and it gave off an abnormal smell. As well as the morbid stench of death lingered the strong scent of paraffin oil. Mr Osborn spoke to Mrs Dawber and she related how the cat, all ablaze, had jumped into her back yard from a certain house in Kemble Street. Ann Coombes was the occupier and she was questioned by the inspector over her suspected involvement. On going into the parlour Mr Osborn spotted a container of paraffin oil precariously sitting by the fire grate. Thankfully, the fire was not lit. In the grate itself he discovered some burnt newspaper and some soot saturated with the same distinctive oil. 'I put some paraffin on a piece of newspaper to drive a strange cat out of the chimney,' said Mrs Coombes, unaware of the terrible outcome her actions brought about.

Before Mr Stewart at the Liverpool Police Court, Ann Coombes was summoned by the RSPCA for cruelty. In answer the woman denied she had coated the cat in paraffin oil, but merely dowsed some paper and lit that. She only wanted to scare the cat out, not kill it. 'Without paraffin oil the most inflammable newspaper would not have produced such conflagration upon the poor cat,' said the magistrate. 'However I don't believe the oil had been put on the cat and would be sorry to think that any adult, much less this woman, would do such a thing.' Considering this was not a deliberate act of cruelty, Mr Stewart dismissed the case from his court. Mrs Coombes had had no conception of the cruel consequences that would arise from her actions and was most sorry for what had happened.

THE DIE-HARD MARKETERS

Today Queen Square is a busy bus stop ferrying shoppers to every corner of the city and afar. This lively workplace of public transport was once an active centre for enterprising stallholders, but the late nineteenth century brought it all to an unwanted end.

On 5 August 1878 approximately forty fruit, vegetable and fish sellers were summoned for causing an obstruction in Queen Square and Great Charlotte Street on various dates since July last. Magistrates Mr Picton and Mr Browning presided.

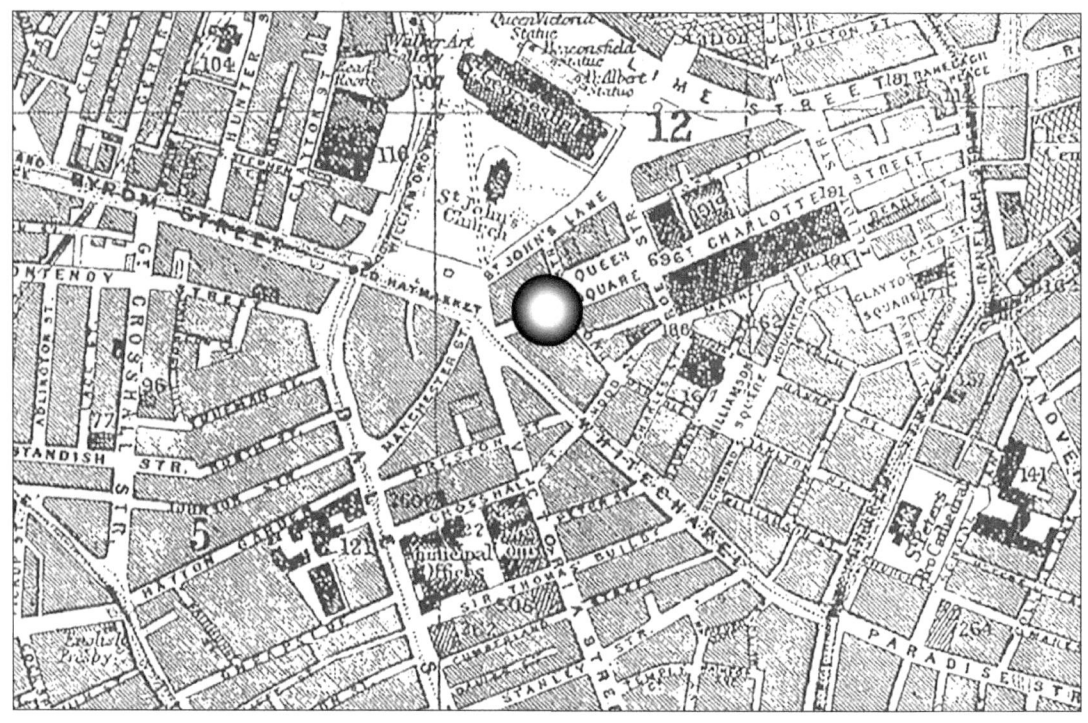

A map of Queen Square from the late nineteenth century.

Queen Square, now a busy bus station.

Mr Picton asked whether or not Great Charlotte Street, situated on the west side of St John's Market, was formerly used and generally recognised as part of the market itself. He was told that there were a great number of people who were in the habit of going there to take up their accustomed spots to trade their wares. The deputy town clerk Mr Atkinson supported this information and recounted the circumstances that had led up to this point. He spoke of how in 1786 under an act of King George III, the Liverpool Corporation had obtained an act through Parliament which allowed them to designate such public parts of the city to use as markets as they saw fit. In 1810, Queen Square and Great Charlotte Street had indeed been designated as such areas. It was not until July last that the market status of those two areas was revoked; a change of which ample notice was given through means of advertisements. 'By this order of the council, Queen Square is no more a market than Bold Street or any other street in the town,' exclaimed Mr Atkinson. 'Anyone exposing goods there created an obstruction just as much as if they did so in Bold Street and were as much liability to penalty.'

Queen Square in the year 1920.

Superintendent Hutchinson of the markets deposed that Queen Square was not a market when he was a boy, but had subsequently been adopted as one and had been seen that way for many years. Mr Little, the manager of St John's Market proved that due notice had been given by the council through advertisements and placards, examples of which were shown to the court. Mr Messenger, a market collector, stated that he had not collected any tolls from any traders from Queen Square or Great Charlotte Street since 5 July.

Dr O'Feeley for the defence alleged that the council ought to have passed not only an order repealing the by-law in regards to the square, but a separate by-law to disband it all together. In response Mr Atkinson said that that course of action had already been taken earlier that year, when the council approved a recommendation from the Market Committee that both places should be discontinued from their previous uses as of 5 July.

The magistrates had heard enough. There could be no excuse for the tradesmen continuing their crafts illegally in places clearly out of bounds. They enforced fines ranging from 5s, 2s and 6d to the forty or so die-hard marketers.

A BIT ON THE SIDE

It had only been a year since seventy-seven-year-old John Faraday wed his wife Mary, but their marital bliss had soon turned sour. In the year 1919, Mrs Faraday took a second bout of legal action against her once dearly beloved and on Thursday 12 June, the couple faced each other at Bootle's Police Court. Mary told the court that a few weeks previously her husband had left her through an unfounded sense of jealously. John resented the fact that she was friends with a man by the name of Mr Lamb who in his opinion was a little too fond of calling.

It was heard that a clock had recently been acquired at the Faraday household and there had been much disagreement over it. Mr Mills Roberts for the defence asked the plaintiff if she had told her husband that Mr Lamb had given her the clock, despite her husband previously giving her money to purchase one.

'Yes,' she answered idly.

'Why did you tell him that?'

'I only said it was a present. There was no harm in it,' said Mrs Faraday.

The magistrate's clerk said that it looked as though Mary was trying to stir up trouble and asked why she would do such a thing.

'Because he always wants to know where I get everything from,' fumed the sixty-one-year-old.

She spoke further about how she had pawned her engagement ring because her husband was always taking it. 'I did it through spite,' Mary admitted. She added that on one or two occasions she had left her husband all day without cooking him any food. Once, John had attempted to destroy the argument-causing clock and two vases, but Mrs Faraday said that she had physically prevented him, but denied kicking him.

'When the case was before the court previously it was adjourned to see if you could not live together?' enquired Mr Mills Roberts.

'Yes, and I agreed,' was her rather sharp reply.

'And one condition made was that you gave Lamb up?'

'Yes'

'And drink?'

'I don't drink!' retorted the elderly woman.

Mrs Faraday then called a witness to support her, but on standing in the witness box, the woman didn't know what to say.

'You say I don't go out at night. You know that very well,' whispered Mary, after creeping to the foot of the stand.

The courtroom laughed at this farcical turn of events.

In his own evidence, John Faraday said that his wife was extravagant. 'She wants me to go! She wants the place free for her fancy man Lamb!'

Once the court managed to suppress their laughter, John continued his tirade upon his wife's 'friend', saying that Lamb was the cause of most of their trouble. Of his wife's first husband, he held deep sympathy.

'I am sorry for the poor man who had to suffer by you for so long. I am afraid he went to his grave with a broken heart.'

The magistrate's clerk intervened. 'You do know a man must keep his wife Mr Faraday?'

'I agree that a man must keep his wife,' replied John, 'but there are exceptions!'

Despite his spouse's troublesome ways, the court ordered Mr Faraday to pay his wife 5s a week for his desertion.

TRAGEDY AT UPHOLLAND

Thirty-five-year-old Elizabeth Williams was a domestic servant from the town of Llanrwst in the Conwy Valley. Up until December 1918, she had lived with her husband, a horse trainer in Wales, but a change of situation had forced Mrs Williams to move to Upholland and take up a position at the Red Lion Hotel. In February she asked her employer, John Marsh, if she could bring her young son to live with her, as she recently had news that her husband had passed away and that there was no one left to care for him. John was rather taken aback at the news, as he was under the impression that Elizabeth was already widowed. The licensee was not normally a sympathetic man, but under the difficult circumstances, Mr Marsh was prepared to make an exception.

He agreed, and Elizabeth and her little three-year-old son John stayed at the pub until July, when Mr Marsh's patience finally ran out. He informed the woman that her services were no longer required, but it was not long before Mr Marsh offered Elizabeth a job working on the farm next door to the Red Lion – on the condition that she did not bring the child with her.

This left Mrs Williams with a serious dilemma. She had no other relatives to turn to, nor could she afford to turn down the job offer. On 24 July she left Upholland taking her son with her. She returned the following day without the toddler, telling Mr Marsh that she had sent him to Oldham to be adopted. During a conversation with her friend Mrs Gaskell about the matter, Elizabeth broke down and began to cry.

'I'm sorry to part with the boy, but he will be with very nice people,' she sobbed. The maid gave a similar explanation to her employer, who was more than happy with the outcome. With no dependencies Elizabeth could work for him without any problems.

However, just four short days later Elizabeth decided to pack her bags and left for Bangor, giving no reason for her sudden departure.

The following day, William Lewis was taking a stroll around the banks of a disused quarry in Digmoor, not far from Upholland, when something horrendous caught his attention. The quarry was flooded to a depth of about 25ft and at the side Mr Lewis spotted the body of a young male floating limply.

Police were informed and an inquest on the youthful corpse was carried out. It was revealed that the child had died from drowning and that he had been in the water for approximately four or five days.

Mrs Williams was tracked down and arrested in Bangor. 'I took off his cap and clogs and dropped him into the water last Thursday,' she admitted tearfully upon arrest. 'I thought of committing suicide but my heart failed me!'

The cap, shoes and a pair of delicately small socks were found in her possession. She was taken to Walton prison, where she was to be incarcerated before her trial. Dr East, the medical officer, found the prisoner to be very depressed and indifferent to his questions. The whole tragic affair was clearly affecting Elizabeth. Nevertheless, she was soon able to relate to police her version of the events that led up to the death of her son in a quite rational manner with no indication of insanity or melancholia.

On Halloween 1919, Elizabeth Williams was brought before Mr Justice Avory at the Liverpool Assizes on a charge of wilful murder. John Marsh, licensee of the Red Lion Hotel, said under cross-examination that he was a widower and admitted intimacy with the accused. He protested that he was under the impression that Mrs Williams was a widow at the time and that she had lied to him.

Defence solicitor Mr Madden argued that Mrs Williams loved her child dearly and pleaded to the jury to find that, broken and overwrought as she was at the time of the tragedy, she was incapable of knowing exactly what she was doing.

The judge stated that if the evidence satisfied the jury – that Mrs Williams had deliberately thrown the boy into the water intending to take away his life and to get rid of it – their duty was to find the accused guilty of murder. They duly returned a guilty verdict.

'It is my painful duty to pass upon the prisoner the full sentence of the law. The recommendation of the jury will be forwarded to the proper quarter where it will receive every consideration,' declared Judge Avory. A solemn sentence of death was then passed and Elizabeth was led below in a state of collapse.

COPPERS IN THE DOCK

The Saturday afternoon of 30 March 1850 witnessed a rather inverted spectacle take place within the city's criminal justice system. John Sherridan and William Page, two Liverpool police officers, were brought to the dock to stand trial on charges of assault.

It was alleged that in the January of that year, John Kilshaw, a timber dealer, had been having a few drinks with friends at a pub in Bankfield Crescent, North Shore. Those within were thoroughly enjoying themselves and the evening was getting merrier by the minute. As time passed the ever-flowing alcohol became too much for some and an unruly fracas duly developed. The police were contacted and soon Constables Sherridan and Page were on the scene with strict instructions to restore order.

Mr Kilshaw left the premises without causing any commotion and headed off towards his lodgings at Banfield Terrace in Kirkdale. He expected the rest of his night to be less eventful than his time at the inn, but John's hopes were, alas, misplaced.

Later that night another resident of Banfield Terrace was awoken by a loud knocking at the front door. Peering through a window and out into the street, the neighbour observed two impatient policemen who continued to hammer hard upon the entrance.

'We are looking for Mr Kilshaw,' an officer announced.

They had reason to believe he had stolen a pocket watch from a sailor in the pub and were keen to investigate.

A neighbour told them the man they were looking for had gone across to check on his timber yard, as he was accustomed to do before going to bed. The officers thanked the informant and left in search of Kilshaw.

It wasn't long before a terrible commotion was heard echoing out from the yard. The neighbour, still intrigued by the inquiry, sought out the origin of the noise and stumbled upon a most dreadful scene of brutality. In the timber yard

PC Sherridan and PC Page were standing over Mr Kilshaw as he rolled about on the ground trying to defend himself from the blows which the officers were inflicting.

'Stab the bugger!' one hollered, as he brought a wooden stick down hard upon their suspect's arm. Mr Kilshaw cried out in agony and the force of the blow broke the makeshift weapon. He suffered further still when the sharp edge of his assailant's cutlass met his brow. That was enough.

Gasps and hushed mutterings were heard from the jury as they listened to the alleged violence.

It was heard how the officers left their victim and walked off heedlessly into the night. Mr Kilshaw was escorted back to his room by the watchful tenant who had seen everything, and soon John found himself under the medical care of Mr Gosling.

The surgeon found the timber-dealer's body to be terribly battered and bruised, and two bleeding scalp wounds bore further witness to the abominable atrocity which had taken place that evening. It would be several days before Mr Kilshaw could even attempt to resume carrying out his business.

That was the case for the prosecution.

Sergeant Wilkins disagreed. He told the court that his officers had visited the public house in Bankfield Crescent on the evening in question. They had received reports of a disturbance, and, sure enough, upon their arrival discovered a row in full flow. He deposed that Mr Kilshaw was dreadfully drunk and attacked the accused several times as they tried to calm the volatile situation. Nevertheless, he alleged that Sheridan and Page allowed him to leave in order to concentrate on the more rowdy individuals.

While carrying out their duty Sergeant Wilkins said that a sailor had informed the constables that he was missing his watch and that he suspected Mr Kilshaw to be the culprit. The officer explained that his men were legally obliged to visit the lodging house where the wanted man was known to reside.

On finding the timber dealer nearby and in the company of a man named Dodd, they went over to ask about the missing watch. It was then, the sergeant stated, that Kilshaw again became violent and struck his officers, as did the man Dodd. It was Kilshaw who withdrew a knife and shouted to stab, the sergeant exclaimed. In consequence of this PC Page advised his colleague to use his cutlass in self-defence. The broken stick spoken of was caused by one of the constables warding off a blow aimed by Dodd, Mr Wilkins attested.

In spite of one or two further witness statements supporting the sergeant's account of Mr Kilshaw's behaviour, the court found in favour of the timber dealer and sentenced the two constables to twelve months imprisonment.

THE PACT

Mary Woods was a hard-working schoolmistress from the town of St Helens. She had been the victim of a paralytic attack when she was very young, but her status of a cripple did not prevent her from living a full and happy life. With her crutch in hand, Mary taught many local children to read and write and made a further wage selling beer from a neighbouring brewery to their parents.

On the night of 28 December 1864, a very close (and sometimes intimate) friend of Miss Woods, Mr James Clitheroe, was drinking at a public house in the area. The conversation there turned to the notorious 'Townley' case, which was the main subject of gossip at the time. 'Next morning there'll be greater bother than ever there had been about Townley,' said James in a pitiful manner. Immediately afterwards witnesses watched him leave the pub and he went round to visit Miss Wood's house.

The precise details of the night from then on are shrouded in mystery, but at about five o'clock a torturous scream was heard to ring out from the school building.

Early the next morning pupils gathered at the school gates anxious to get inside away from the bitter winter winds. It was unusual for the gates still to be locked at this hour, but the small crowd waited patiently expecting Miss Woods to come to greet them at any moment. It wasn't long before a man named Mounsell started to lose his patience. He decided to venture to the side entrance to see what the delay was. 'Miss Woods?' he called out irritably. There was no reply. Mr Mounsell pushed open the unlocked side door and carefully walked up the stairs. 'Miss Woods?' he called out again. This was all very strange. The schoolmistress was never late and could only be described as a credit to her profession.

Mr Mounsell walked slowly into Miss Woods' bedroom – where he finally discovered her. The woman was lying in bed with her throat sliced open.

The blood which had once gushed forth in frenzy had dried hard. Next to her hand there sat a blood-stained razor and above the bed a large and bloody handprint was embossed onto the wall. Miss Jones was not the only victim amongst this vivid vista of death: also on the bed lay James Clitheroe. The twenty-two-year-old was not dead, but he had clearly attempted to take his own life. He had three grisly wounds upon his bristled neck which steadily trickled to his chest.

Mr Mounsell called for the police and officers were soon at the school.

'We made it up to cut our throats. She told me that the razor was in the drawer under the looking glass,' gasped James. 'I fetched the razor, got into bed and first cut my throat.'

Mr Clitheroe was put into the care of a surgeon who treated his brutal self-mutilation. With careful care he was able to make a decent recovery and was forced to stand trial at the South Lancashire Assizes on 22 March. James was a man of small stature and had a pale look of nervousness about him as he stood before the court. The particulars of the events were read out and it seemed that some sort of suicide pact had been agreed between the prisoner and the deceased.

Mr Higgins for the prosecution submitted the view that if two persons agreed to kill themselves and one was unsuccessful the one who survived was, by law, guilty of murder. However, he had another view of the case. Miss Woods had saved and scraped together upwards of £30 worth of savings. Mr Clitheroe knew of this and knew where it was kept. The court also heard how when the prisoner was in the charge of an officer, he mentioned to a colleague that they had to purchase some milk. James happily directed the policemen to search Mary's pockets, where he said that they would find three halfpence in copper. It seemed to Mr Higgins that James had a suspiciously good knowledge of Miss Woods' finances.

Mr Lawton lived nearby to the scene of the crime. He took to the stand and recalled that he had left for work at about five o'clock on the Monday morning in question when he heard a female cry of 'oh don't!'

Mr Higgins further said that Mr Clitheroe's statement that he and the deceased had agreed to kill themselves was untrue: it was his view that, in all probability, Clitheroe had cut Miss Woods' throat at about five o'clock in the morning and that she must have been dead for some hours before he decided to cut his own throat.

Mr Torr then addressed the jury, but his rather weak defence was worthless. He could only suggest that the defendant lacked a motive.

Mr Justice Willes had heard enough. He directed the jury to retire and return a verdict. After a brief absence they returned from their consultation with the fate-sealing word of 'guilty'.

His Lordship placed the black cap upon his head and, in tones scarcely audible over James Clitheroe's hollowing, passed a sentence of death. The condemned man was removed from court in a most pitiful condition and felt the hangman's rope on 16 April.

DEATH OF A SWEETHEART

In the year 1895 Sarah Jenkinson was employed as a domestic servant to a couple residing at 2 Godwin Street, Liverpool and had been for about three years. She was courting a man by the name of Edward O'Brien. He was a labourer and former member of the militia corps but had not long been discharged.

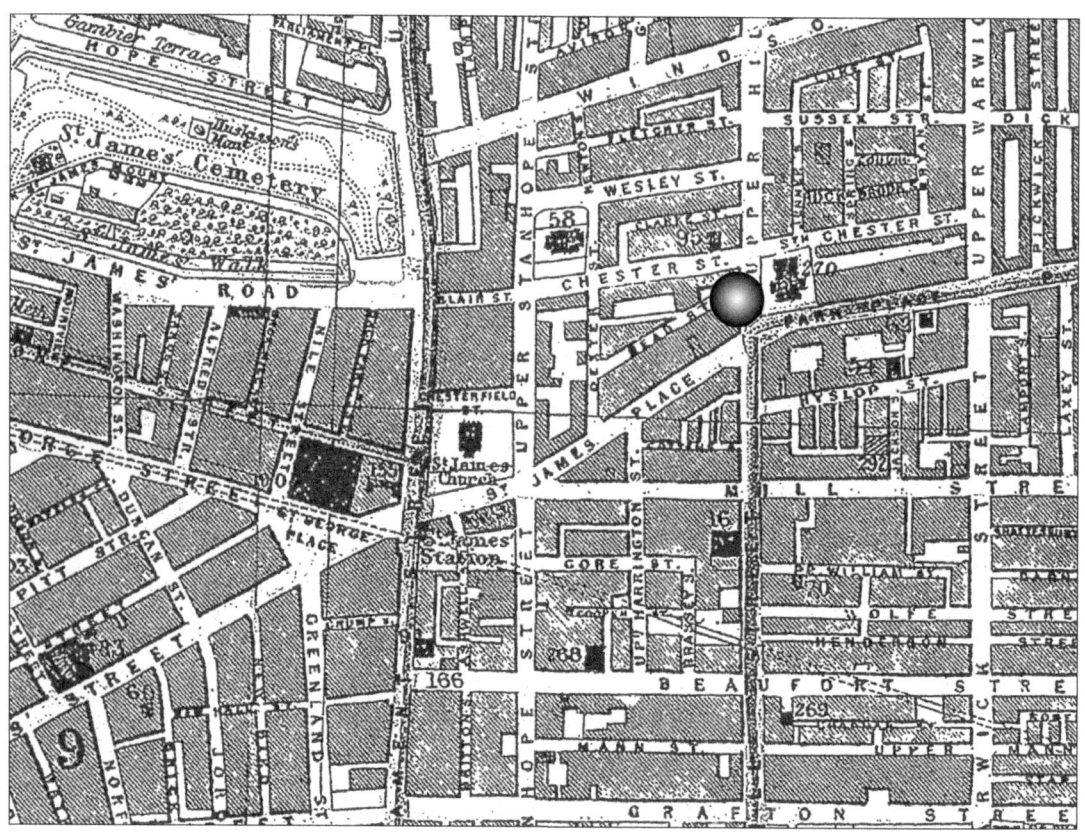

The vicinity of Upper Parliament Street, from a map, c. 1890.

On the afternoon of 29 July the couple, her employer and some neighbours descended on a beerhouse in Godwin Street for a few hours of alcoholic hilarity. Amongst the group of drinkers was Mrs Fitzsimmons. In her pocket sat a cased razorblade she had taken from her house to hide from her volatile husband. While taking a handkerchief out of her pocket, Mrs Fitzsimmons dropped the case onto the floor. Edward O'Brien was quick to bend down and pick up the shaving blade. 'I'll take care of this for you,' remarked Edward politely. He looked over to his girlfriend and joked, in rather poor taste, 'What would you say if I cut your throat?' No notice was taken of Edward's dark sense of humour and the day continued happily until five o'clock, when the money finally ran out.

It was then that a sense of dismay overcame the party. Where was the next drink going to come from? O'Brien had an idea: he left the pub in double-time and headed off to the nearest pawn shop. The man's coat was soon pawned in return for some quick cash and Edward returned eagerly and triumphantly called for booze. The relationship between Mr O'Brien and Miss Jenkinson must have suffered a blow, as later that evening Sarah left the pub in anger. Edward followed her out and spotted her up the road near to her place of work. 'If you don't come down the street it will be worse for you!' he shouted rather publicly. The irritated maid ignored her boyfriend's threats and headed up to No. 2. Susannah Nesbitt let her in and led the slightly drunken woman to the staircase up to her room.

It was only a minute or two later that a hard knocking was delivered to the property's front door.

'Is … is Sally there?' Hiccupped Edward, supported by the doorpost.

'I'm afraid not,' answered Mrs Chesters, the homeowner, 'she's gone out.'

'Just open the door and let me have a word with her,' he pleaded.

'Sorry, she went out.'

O'Brien was forced to accept this (somewhat basic) cover story and staggered off down the road. Ten minutes later he saw Mrs Chesters scurry across to a neighbour's, so he headed back to the house once more to find his girlfriend. Again, he knocked on the front door – then finding it unlocked he ran up the stairs and broke down the door to Sarah's room. The drunkard grabbed hold of the woman and roughly dragged her down the stairs in front of the whole household. By the torn neck of her dress he pulled Sarah into the hallway with one hand, while reaching into his pocket with the other.

Those inside shouted to Mrs Chesters to come back to the house at once, and she hurried into the crowded passage. She saw her servant clutching a ginger beer bottle in one hand and trying to shove Edward away, but he refused to release his hold. Mrs Chesters had had enough. She grabbed a tight hold of O'Brien's wrist and turned her gaze to the kitchen to call for assistance. However, when she turned back she was greeted by a horrible sight: a stream of blood was spurting rhythmically from Sarah's neck. Mrs Chesters watched in horror as Sarah staggered through the kitchen and out in the back yard. Two cuts had been inflicted upon her throat which had penetrated right down to the spinal column, severing the principal arteries, veins and windpipe. 'My God! He has killed me,' Sarah gasped softly, before collapsing to the concrete. The entire household fell silent; they could not believe what they had just witnessed. Even the stoic Edward, who left the house – followed by John Gillard – as if his feelings had been anesthetised was affected: once outside, the labourer broke down and he began to cry uncontrollably. 'Oh Jack, what have I done?'

'Sally's dead!' yelled Gillard.

'Oh Lord, have mercy on me! Oh my mother!' screamed Edward. He was very drunk, and beside himself with grief. O'Brien walked towards the corner of Embeldon Street where he spotted a blacksmith with whom he was acquainted. 'I have done it Jack; stick to me,' he cried. O'Brien handed over the bloodied razor and a knife.

Suddenly the calmness of the night was broken by the sharp sounds of police whistles. Time was up. Detective Sergeant Morrison arrested the crimson-covered man and directed him to the station. The snivelling was relentless. 'Well, I have done it. I am very sorry. It is all through drink,' Edward cried.

Mr O'Brien was ultimately sent to the assizes for his crime. At St George's Hall on 25 November, the twenty-six-year-old pleaded not guilty to the murder of his sweetheart, Sarah Jenkinson.

Catherine Jenkinson of Harold Street, mother of the deceased, gave evidence as to the relationship between the accused and her daughter. She said that she had never heard Sarah utter one bad thing about Edward and as far as she knew, he was always very kind to her.

George Piggot stated he and the prisoner were members of the Liverpool Regiment of Militia and were discharged at Warrington on 27 July. Mr Piggot spoke of how he, Edward, Sarah and another woman were drinking on the day in question. Later, at about 10.30 p.m., the witness went to No. 2 Godwin Street and saw O'Brien grappling with the deceased before seeing blood shoot forth from her throat.

Under cross-examination, George said that O'Brien had been drinking more or less all day, and Miss Jenkinson had a drop or two as well.

Peter Brogan, Mary's son Robert Chesters, and Ernest Parker also testified, with the latter remarking that he had heard Sarah call out that the prisoner had killed her. It was the opinion of the three men that Edward had always been on good terms with Sarah, who in fact had herself been known to become raucous under the influence of drink.

Emma Bunnett was next to take the stand, dressed in her Salvation Army uniform. She alleged that she visited the house on the Monday night at about 10 p.m. Emma confirmed that she had also seen the prisoner grab hold of Miss Jenkinson by the neck of her dress and act in a most brutal manner towards her.

Medical evidence showed that Sarah Jenkinson's throat had been cut in two places and great violence must have been used. It would have been impossible for the woman to shout for help.

Dr Beamish was called to give evidence at the request of Edward O'Brien. He was the surgeon at Walton Gaol and he revealed that there were three depressions on the right side of the prisoner's skull. 'Such persons were more susceptible to alcohol than ordinary people,' alleged the doctor.

After hearing all the evidence the judge began summing up the case. He reminded the jury that the razor was in the prisoner's trouser pocket: how could the weapon have got out of his pocket if he had not taken it out himself? 'And what did he take it out for?' questioned His Lordship.

The jury – without even leaving their box to consider their verdict – found Edward O'Brien guilty of wilful murder.

'Do you have anything to say?' O'Brien was asked.

There was no answer.

'Edward O'Brien, yours is one more melancholy instance of the effects of drink in this city. I will not be cruel enough to keep you in suspense before I pronounce upon you the sentence of the law.'

The death sentence was then passed upon O'Brien, who showed little emotion or feeling.

'Can I speak?' asked Edward unexpectedly. 'May I have my body and head examined at the infirmary?'

His Lordship took no notice of this surprising request, forcing O'Brien to continue his bizarre demands. 'When I am hanged and finished with, will you let my body and head be examined and put it in the paper what is to do with my head?'

The court remained in silence as the prisoner was led quietly down the steps to the cells to await his capital punishment.

MADAM BRENNAN

At about 7 p.m. of 9 October 1903, two women hurried to a house in Thomaston Street, just off Netherfield Road. They were keen not to be seen and gave a rapid knock on the door. After a few moments of anxious waiting a young girl answered.

'Is the fortune teller in?' asked one of the women, coyly. The noise of the latch being removed echoed in the hallway, and then the door creaked open. The ladies were shown into a dimly lit back room where they saw two other

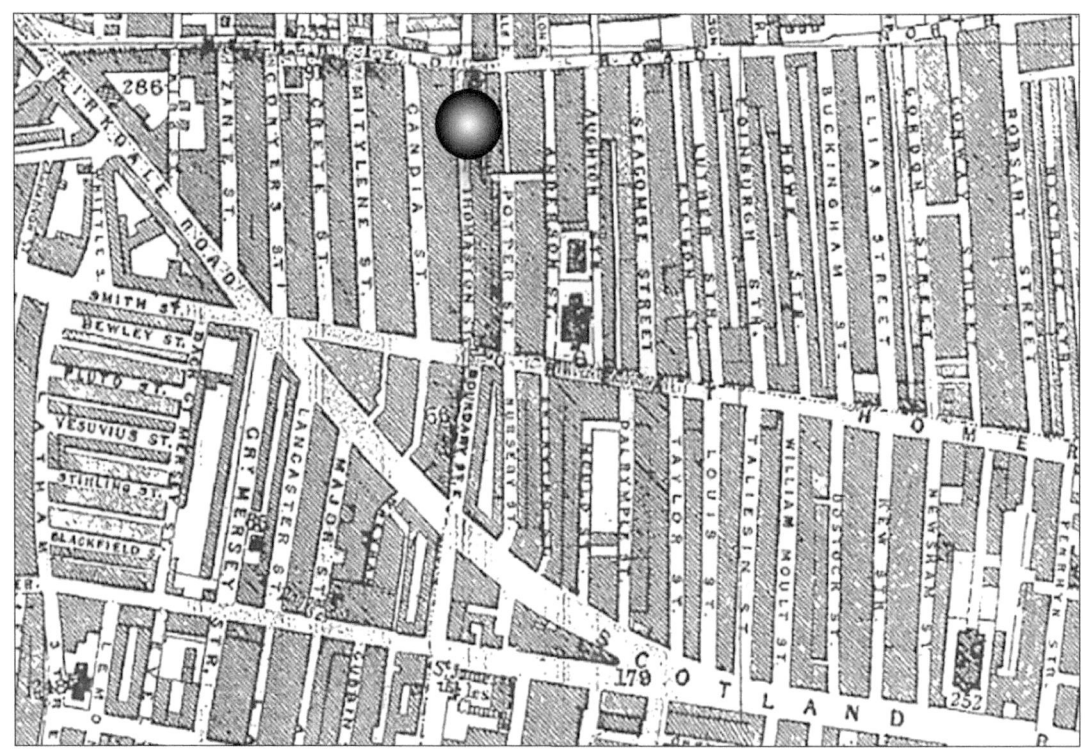

The mystic's abode, Thomaston Street as seen on a map, c. 1900.

women were sitting at a small table. On the table were a number of cards, each one printed with various colourful images. Mary Brennan was a well-known seer in the neighbourhood, and she invited her new guests to take a seat. Mary collected up the cards and handed them over to one of the women to shuffle. This she did, and the cards were carefully handed back to the mysterious Madam Brennan. She breathed heavily as she laid the cards out one by one. 'You shall be a widow, but you will have two offers of marriage,' Mary said with a marvellous air of intrigue. 'Your husband is given to drink,' was Mary's next remarkable insight, 'and you have nine children, one of whom will be soon be married.'

At that point three more women entered the room, while more waited in the lobby. Mary Brennan's abilities certainly appeared to be in high demand. The thankful woman reached into her purse and paid the psychic 6d. 'If it had been in Bold Street that would have been five shillings,' smiled Mary, grateful for the payment. The second woman proceeded to have her fortune told. The cards were again shuffled and again laid out upon the table. 'The cards say that you are single,' said Mary. The lady shook her head, much to the bemusement of the fortune teller. 'Then the young man you are with is no good. You are to give him up as there is a better one waiting for you.' The woman looked slightly unsure, but nevertheless also paid Madam Brennan the sum of 6d and thanked her for her services.

On the night of the 16th, the two friends returned to Thomaston Street for a second reading. Just as before, the pair were shown into the back room to await their turn. Before them were three other women who each paid 3d for their divination. The trio soon left and it was not long before Madam Brennan got to work on her next set of visitors. The mystic foretold that one of the ladies would soon end up a widow and that a financial settlement would come to pass in the near future. She also predicted that her second husband was also to be a widower, that he was dark and that he had already purchased a ring to give to her. 'You shall live long and die happy,' exclaimed Mary.

Now it was time for the second guest to be told her fate. In this reading the cards foresaw her meeting up with her boyfriend and settling a quarrel they had supposedly been having. Marriage would soon follow, but if he did not propose then she was to leave him, as marriage was to be with another who was waiting to wed.

'What a load of nonsense,' thought the woman. She had had her doubts about the first reading, but this was ridiculous. Her friend paid for the session at a cost of 1s 6d for herself and 6d for the other.

The now uninhabited area of land where Madam Brennan 'foretold fortunes'.

'I don't do this for a living,' remarked Madam Brennan. 'There is no standard fee as such.'

The pair left, and, after discussing what they had been told, they considered themselves to have been conned. They contacted the police and Mary Brennan was brought before the City Police Court to face magistrates. The two women gave evidence of their dealings with Madam Brennan and damned her as nothing more than a clever con artist.

'We only do it to oblige people!' Brennan protested.

'If you had been able to tell fortunes you would have been able to tell that you would have been here today,' laughed Magistrate Steward, before fining her 40s plus costs.

A MEASURABLE OFFENCE

On 26 February 1869, Superintendent Martin, an inspector of weights and measures, made his way to a property in Princess Street, Waterloo. He was joined by his assistant Myers, and Sergeant Price, knocking on the door with a hard swift tap. After a few seconds of waiting, Miss Helen Doubleday opened the door. 'We've come to inspect your measures,' announced Mr Martin. 'I'm sorry, she's not in,' replied Helen, with a slight tone of nervousness.

'You can show the measures to me, I suppose.'

'She's not in sir. I'm sorry.'

The inspector was perplexed at the woman's resistance, so asked her sternly, but politely, one final time.

'Oh – the measures!' exclaimed Miss Doubleday. 'I thought you said the Mrs.'

Helen opened the door fully and stepped aside to let the men in. Immediately Mr Martin saw the lady of the house, Charlotte Ashcroft, get up from her seat and hurry to an adjoining room. 'Go and see what she is up to, Myers,' ordered the official, while he and the sergeant continued on to the kitchen. Not even a minute passed before sounds of verbal abuse could be heard coming from the next room.

'You're a scamp!' raged Mrs Ashcroft. 'I will not have such low rascals about my place!' The young apprentice was soon saved from the furious female when Mr Martin bravely entered the room. 'What's the matter here?' he asked, authoritatively.

Thomas Myers said he was trying to examine some measures but the woman was making a nuisance of herself. The inspector walked towards the counter where there stood between eight and twelve measures, each filled high with cream. 'I'll need to examine these, Mrs Ashcroft. Could you empty them please?'

'I'll do no such thing. You do it.'

Superintendent Martin reached over to grab a soup bowl from a rack and began to scoop the creamy contents out into the dish. Upon emptying the third measure, Mrs Ashcroft grabbed hold of the two he had emptied. 'Before you look at these I shall throw them in the ashpit,' she grimaced. Myers grabbed her hand and took one of the drained measures from the woman's grasp before she had a chance to rush outside. Charlotte was soon in the back yard and was about to open the door to the ashpit when Mr Martin called out. 'Don't!' he shouted, and he went over, knocking the can from her hand. At this point Henry Ashcroft, Charlotte's husband, arrived home. The couple did not get on well at all, and amongst the mayhem Charlotte turned her attentions to her husband: 'This is my house and you have no business here at all!' screeched the livid wife. Mr Myers and Mr Martin carried on with their duty and managed to successfully inspect the measures. The former made hurriedly scribbled notes regarding the conduct of Charlotte Ashcroft which would form the basis of the prosecution that she would now face. When Mr Ashcroft, a milk dealer, was eventually allowed to enter the house, he was immediately spoken to by the superintendent. Mr Martin said he was sorry, but he would have to summon him for having two unstamped measures and his wife for obstructing him in the execution of his duty.

At Basnett Street Court the Aschcrofts were brought before magistrates to be tried for their offences. The pair of illegal measures were produced and the conduct of Mrs Ashcroft was recalled. In her defence, Charlotte said that when she was going to the ashpit she was merely going to empty the contents into it, not the vessels themselves. She further stated that the cans did not belong to her at all, but to her children – despite the obvious fact that there were about ten cans and only two children.

Mr Myers corroborated with the inspector and affirmed that Mr Martin had been perfectly civil to the defendant, as did Sergeant Price. Mr James, barrister on behalf of the accused, raised the point that his clients were not bound to have their measures stamped unless they were liable to being deficient, and this was not the case. Mr James also called Miss Doubleday, sister of Charlotte, as a witness. She said that the so-called illegal cans had never been used as measures.

The magistrates listened to her protective prose, but it was no use. They found Mr Ashcroft guilty of having two illegal measures in his possession and imposed a fine of 20s. Luckily for his wife, the summons laid against her was mercifully ignored.

A QUESTION OF SANITY

In the February of 1850, twenty-seven-year-old Mary Powell was brought to the Liverpool workhouse at Brownlow Hill. She was suffering from serious problems of the mind and was placed in the institution's lunatic asylum. In time, she made excellent progress in recovering her senses and was allowed out of the asylum and into the main house. There staff put her to work in the nursery where Mary seemed most competent, conducting herself with the greatest decorum. She was the mother of three children herself, two of which, Mary and Edward, were eventually brought to live with her by Mrs Graham, Mary's sister.

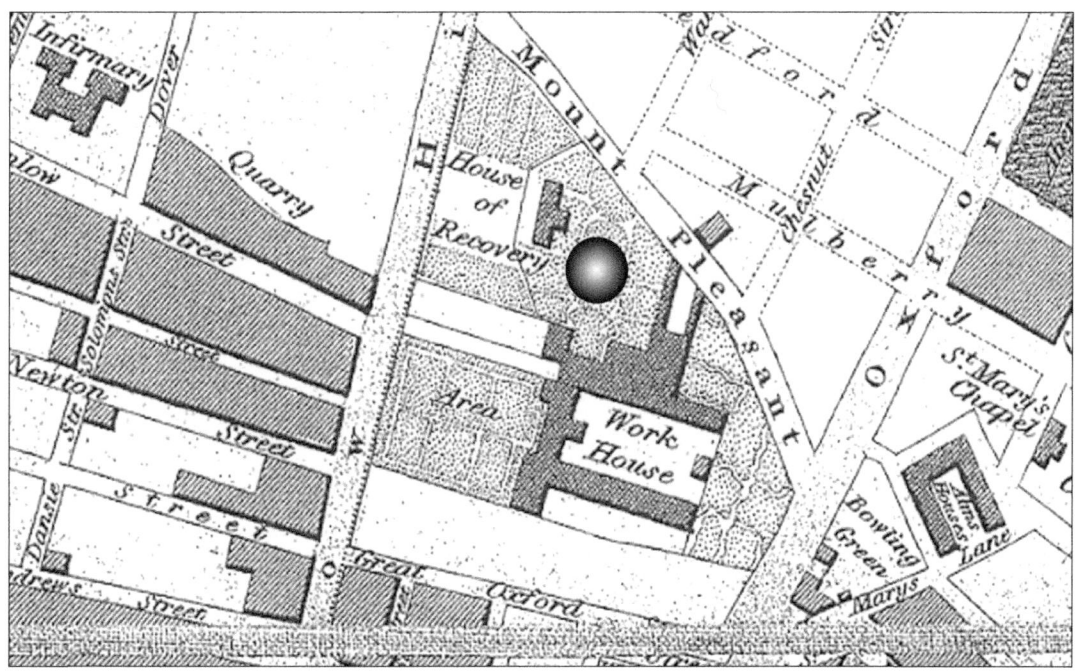

The workhouse depicted in the early 1800s.

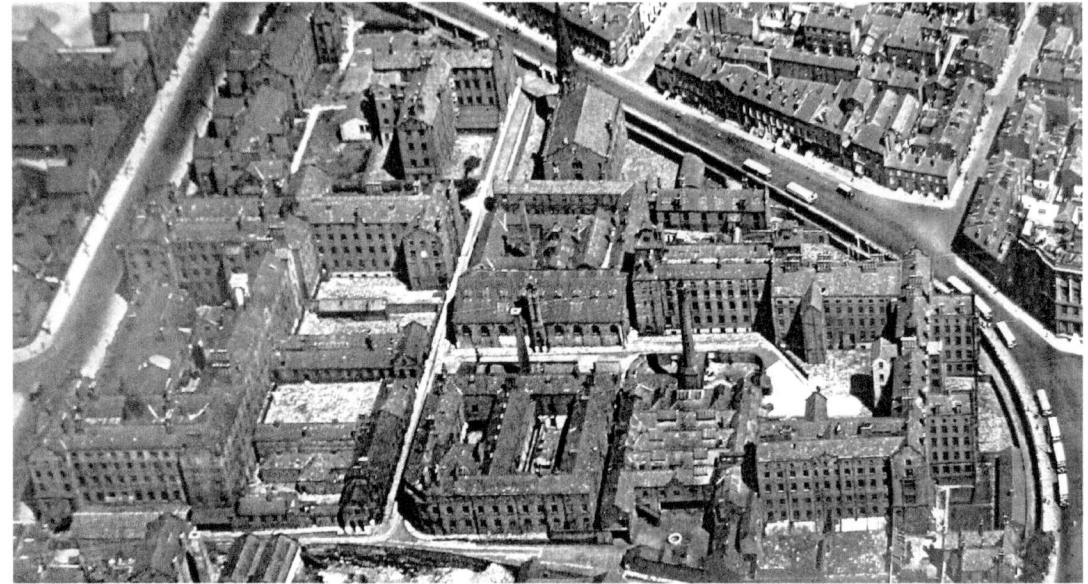
An early twentieth-century aerial view of Brownlow Hill.

Four months passed with Mrs Powell seeming quite *compus mentis*. There was little sign of the awful derangement that had first brought her into the asylum. One afternoon her husband visited and demanded Mary and the kids leave at once. She refused, screeching to nurses that he only wanted to ill use her and that she had to stay. She protested that she had run away from Mr Powell due to his abuse and that she and the children were not safe with him. Edward Gray, the assistant overseer, was called for, and he spoke to Mr Powell about the situation. He calmly told him that he had ordered the family be sent back into the house as it was in their best interests and that he was not to call again. The news sent Mary's husband into a rage – in fact, he became so violent that a policeman had to forcibly remove him from the premises. 'Gleeson Wilson has been hung,' he told the constable with a glare. 'Perhaps I'll be next.' Powell then threatened to break the officer's neck, therefore landing himself a cell in the Bridewell. The next day he was brought before magistrates and sentenced to a month of imprisonment for his intimidating behaviour.

On 10 June, Mr Powell returned to the workhouse and again asked to see his wife and children. This time he told officials that he was planning to head to America and wished to say goodbye. Mr Gray politely – but sternly – declined.

A few days later Mary came to the assistant overseer's office and begged to be let out to see her husband. She had heard of her husband's transatlantic ambition and wanted to meet with him for one last time. It was a long while before she could be persuaded to stay put, and she was repeatedly reminded of the domestic hell that he had put her through. Mr Gray did not see Mrs Powell again until 17 July when she came into his office with house bookkeeper Mr Heathcoat's errand boy. 'Mr Heathcoat has sent me to be discharged for a few hours,' said Mary. She needed Edward's permission to be taken off the books and then to be re-admitted in the evening. Mr Gray sighed. 'Please, don't go out at all,' he said. He knew her brute of a husband would still be in the city and was afraid that she would fall foul of his abusive ways again. This time though Mary could not be persuaded. She pleaded for a ticket to leave and, as she was adamant. She was allowed out. The inmate left the workhouse at about half-past three that afternoon, taking her children with her.

Mary headed off to her sister's house, who was most surprised to see her. Mrs Powell spoke of her plans to meet with her husband to discuss looking after the children. Mary spoke quite rationally, but Mrs Graham still entertained some misgivings as to her state of mind. She left the house and was not seen again until eight o'clock that night, when Mary was spotted in Bath Street carrying a partially clothed baby in her arms. The passer-by called over to her and haughtily advised that she should take better care of the child. Mary just laughed, and appeared either drunk or insane. The good Samaritan attempted to follow her, but Mrs Powell was too quick and was out of sight in a matter of minutes.

A short while afterwards the body of a small girl was found on some warehouse steps in Lancelot's Hey. The child had been strangled with the string that still sat tight around its tiny neck. Mary, however, had run wildly through the streets, ending up at the ferry landing stage. She looked down towards the gushing waters of the Mersey. In an instant, witnesses watched as the woman hurled herself into the river in a hysterical bid for death. It was with great difficulty that she was rescued by plucky port staff and brought back to dry land. Mary was conveyed to the Northern Hospital where she at once raised concerns with her unusual conduct. She seemed very distressed and accused herself of being a murderer. Doctors ordered her to be sent back to the workhouse – where staff were horrified to learn of Mrs Powell's gruesome self-allegations. She declared herself killer of her two children and sobbed that she had left one in a privy in Burlington Street. 'I can't remember what I did with the other.'

Police Inspector Stephen Haines was contacted and he spoke with the accused regarding her statements. She told him her name and mentioned that she was

The Metropolitan Cathedral now sits at location of the workhouse.

a married woman who had left her husband due to his abusive attitude. Mary added that she had been living at the workhouse where the staff had been very good to her. In regards to her children, there was no doubt as to their fate. 'I strangled them with a pinafore. My hands have done the deed.'

Once tried and found guilty by magistrates, Mary Powell was brought before the next assizes. She climbed meekly into the dock and cried bitterly as she acknowledged her guilt. Mary was given a chair and sat tearfully before an expressionless judge and jury.

The surgeon of the workhouse gave evidence about the prisoner's state of mind upon entering the institution. He said that she would frequently complain of her husband's appalling treatment and would burst into a frenzy whenever his name was mentioned.

The doctor stated that on being taken back to the workhouse Mary made several attempts to escape – presumably to try and take her own life.

Mr Thomas Chalmer, the gaol surgeon, had studied the prisoner's mental state and he considered her sane at present; however, he added that there was no proof as to whether she was sane at the time of the deaths.

Several further witnesses gave evidence, including workhouse nurse Catherine McCormick, workhouse inmate Eliza Pullard, Mrs Graham, Mr Heathcoat and Mr Gray. All truthfully related their experiences with the accused and each gave the impression that Mary was not well at all.

The judge in summing up drew attention to the ultimate question. Was Mrs Powell insane at the time she murdered the two children or did she carry out the dreadful acts in sound mind? Mary Powell was found to be insane and was ordered to be to be detained indefinitely at her majesty's pleasure.

A REMARKABLE CAPTURE

One morning in September 1877, an extraordinary incident took place at Liverpool's famous landing stage. Early that month a teenager from a well-to-do family left his Shrewsbury home without a word of warning. Naturally, his mother was left inconsolable at his sudden departure and pleaded for her elder son to go off and find him.

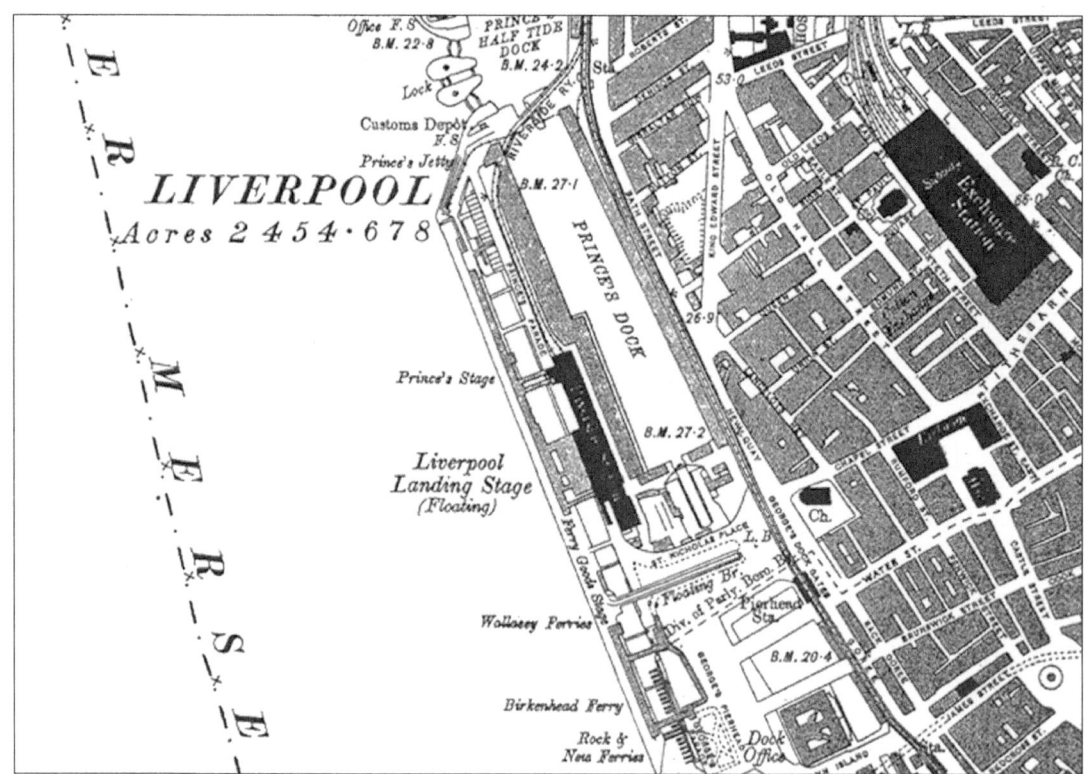

An Edwardian map showing the landing stage where the boy was remarkably captured.

The brother first travelled to Manchester to visit some friends and asked if they had heard from the young wanderer. With no success, he ventured to nautical Liverpool. The lad had never shown an interest in a seafaring career, but there was always the possibility that he had fallen in with a crowd who did. If this was so, Liverpool was the place to be. 18 September saw the man search high and low, questioning all who may have caught even a fleeting glimpse of his lost sibling. Again his quest came to nothing, leaving the family at a loss as to what to do next.

A friend suggested that a visit to Birkenhead's Cathcart House might yield some information. He was told that runaway boys were known to sometimes seek refuge there. Next day the elder brother made his way down to the windy landing stage to sail to the peninsula. The boat to Woodside had not yet made its return trip so he waited patiently alongside a gathering of other would-be river-crossers. A conversation soon arose between him, the landing stage manager John King, and Police Constable Gradwell. They exchanged the usual pleasantries regarding the weather and such, but it was not long before the chat turned to the missing boy.

'What sort of lad is he?' prompted Mr King, stroking his chin.

'He's about seventeen and wears a round pilot reeting jacket and a billycock hat,' answered the Shropshireman. 'He has light brown hair and walks very upright.'

'Indeed,' mused Mr King. He turned his gaze from the water and casually looked towards a small bookstall a few yards back. 'Officer,' continued the stage master, 'keep a lookout for such a lad as the one described'. Before the constable could reply to the somewhat high-handed order, a youth approached the book stall and began browsing through the day's newspapers.

'If we should see him, is that youth anything like him?' interrupted Mr King. The man turned, quite unconcerned, and looked towards the boy now being pointed at. He did a double-take, and, shaking his head in disbelief, shouted, 'It's him! It's him!' Crowds were compelled to adopt cat-like reflexes as the elder brother darted through the mass to lay a firm pair of imprisoning hands upon the lad's arm. The remarkable detection momentarily stunned him, but upon realising his capture he tried in vain to escape the tight-fisted hold. The truant struggled for several minutes before his strength finally faded. A hansom cab was hailed and the two brothers climbed inside. No doubt the boy's forcible return to Shrewsbury was a relief to all but him.

THE CHOCOLATE BOX

In Liverpool's Lime Street there once stood a certain café often frequented by young men and young ladies. The Chocolate Box, as it was known, was owned by John Canevali and his wife Maud. The café consisted of three rooms all fitted with the usual tables and chairs where customers would sit to grab a light snack, a cup of coffee or, as a shocked magistrate heard, a prostitute.

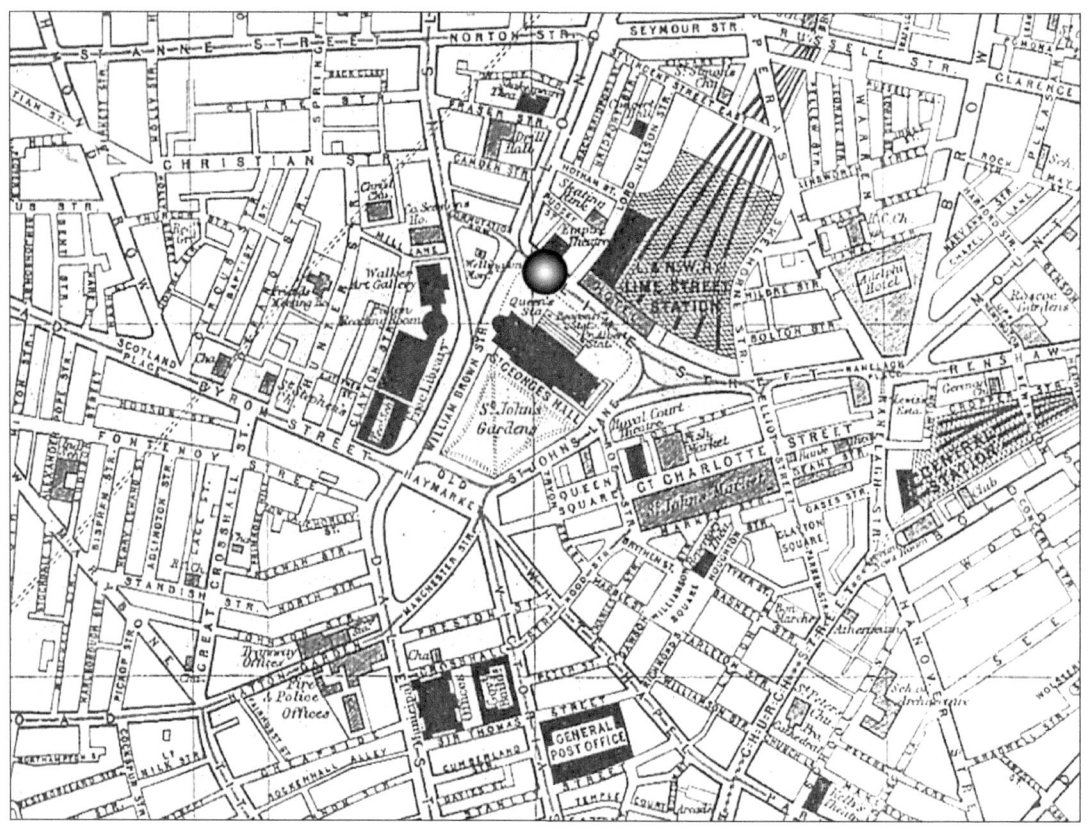

One of Liverpool's most recognised addresses: Lime Street, as shown on a map from 1924.

Liverpool's Lime Street approximately a century ago.

At the police court on 22 October 1919, Mr and Mrs Canevali along with their manageress Ethel Taylor were charged with permitting lowly women to ply their trade at the establishment.

The police had been keeping the property under close surveillance on the night of 22 September. Between eight and eleven o'clock, officers counted no less than sixty-five women aged between fifteen and twenty in the café. Among them were eleven ladies of a certain profession who were each seen to leave with a male in tow. It was unusual for these girls to stay and have anything to eat; they came for the transatlantic sailors who would drink at the American Bar just up the street. Detective Sergeant Alexander deposed in court to witnessing a steady stream of drunken lads falling in and out of the Chocolate Box and inside watching an unruly display of intoxicate dancing. The detective recalled how he made his way around to the rear of the café where he heard some disgustingly obscene language being spoken without shame. On another night of surveillance, he saw 'customers' openly kissing the girls and allowing them to

Liverpool's Lime Street as seen in 2008.

sit on their knees. In three or four instances sailors were seen to commit indecent acts. It was nothing less than a vista of vulgarity. On exiting the shop he heard one fellow remark, 'You can always get a girl if you go to the Chocolate Box.'

In answer to the charges Mr Canevali protested that he was not at the premises on the nights described. Still, as the licence holder, the law stated that he was responsible for enforcing suitable conduct within his business.

In all there were twenty-two members of the public who spoke against the immoral debauchery permitted to take place within the rooms. Conversely, the Canevalis usually bore an excellent character. John owned a second restaurant over on the Wirral which coupled as the family home and Maud often took over the running of the café when needed. It was she who was in charge on the nights in question, but she claimed to be unaware of any prostitutes on the premises.

In summing up, the magistrate felt quite satisfied that the staff at the Chocolate Box were indeed quite oblivious to the prostitutes working inside. On the other hand, disorderly conduct had without doubt taken place, and for that a weighty fine of £16 was imposed. It is presumed Mr and Mrs Canevali began to keep a closer eye on the quality of their customers, and their antics, from then on.

THE MUMMY OF HOPE PLACE

Inspector Morgan was a sanitary official and at about 10.30 a.m. on 1 July 1884, he called at a house in Hope Place, just off Pilgrim Street. Number 22 was his destination and as was his usual custom for this address, he went around to the back to examine the water closet. He tried the door. It was locked. The man knocked hard and called out, but there was no answer. This was most odd, and Mr Morgan supposed something was amiss. Under the hustle and bustle of everyday commotion, the inspector could just about hear

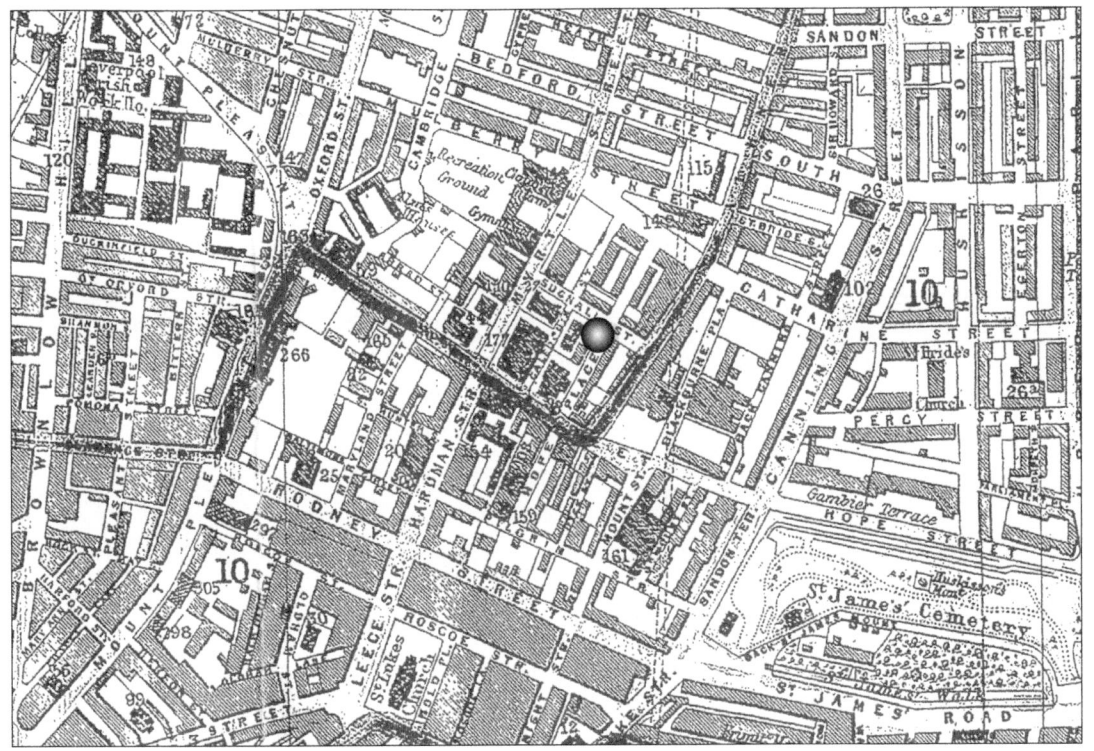

Hope Place, where Mrs Wallace was discovered. Map, c. 1890.

The charming façade of 22 Hope Place, 2008.

a quiet but baffling buzz. He gave one last shout in case the owner, the elderly Mrs Wallace, had perhaps been caught short and was using the toilet, before he decided to force the door. After some difficulty the inspector eventually managed to open the closet, and inside he found Frances Wallace. She was dead, and an awful sour scent enveloped the whole yard as a swarm of buzzing flies flew out towards him.

Police Constable 1129 was sent for and he duly arrived at the property to investigate the pitifully ugly circumstance. Mrs Wallace was decomposing on the filthy urine-soaked floor of the closet with a small satchel left sitting on the seat. The constable contacted his colleagues back at the station and witnesses were sought to formally identity the body. Mrs Ernest, wife of an engine fitter living at 101 Cockburn Street, Toxteth had known Frances Wallace for about twelve years. She informed police that she was a widow and that she used to earn a small living serving. When not at work, Frances was said to indulge in a drop to drink, sometimes going on bouts lasting for several days. This testimony was backed up by a second acquaintance, Mrs Burgess, who further added that Mrs Wallace was in the habit of taking things that did not belong to her. The velvet jacket she was found wearing, and the unmistakable satchel located nearby, left no doubt to either of the women that the body was that of Frances Wallace. This was not the case for the deceased's own unemployed son, who when asked whether the decayed deceased was in fact his mother, was unable to confirm.

Dr Paull, a medical officer from the Royal Infirmary, made a thorough examination of the woman but he found it virtually impossible to ascertain an exact cause of death, not least due to the absence of internal organs. Mrs Wallace had deteriorated to nothing more than a mass of dried muscle and skin, practically mummified. On opening her skull Dr Paull found a horrific nest of dead but well-fed bluebottles. At an inquest the following Saturday an open verdict was returned. Dr Paull said that he was inclined to believe that Frances died from an apoplectic fit and had been dead for a considerable period of time.

AN UNFORTUNATE HURRY

June 18 1878 saw the inquest into the tragic death of Adline Alcide take place before Mr Aspinall, the Liverpool Coroner. Adline was the stepdaughter of John Boyle, a master mariner who along with the rest of his family resided at 141 Stanley Road. The girl was only ten years of age, and on Friday 14 June she was busy helping her mother by counting some copper coins saved in a cabinet. Her young, curious brother had decided not to help with the counting and instead scavenged the cabinet for more interesting items. A revolver, his father's, was found, and he held the weapon with glee. 'Adie I will shoot you,' joked the child, and he pointed the gun towards his elder sister. Before Mrs Boyle had a chance to turn, the revolver was fired and Adline fell screaming into her arms. Amidst a chorus of crying Mrs Boyle contacted a doctor, but he said that he would not be able to attend in time. Indeed, with time being of the essence, the wounded girl was taken to the Stanley Hospital for immediate assistance. There doctors successfully removed a single bullet from Aldine's neck, but it looked unlikely that there would be a happy ending. Professional opinion proved correct, and the girl passed away the following Saturday morning.

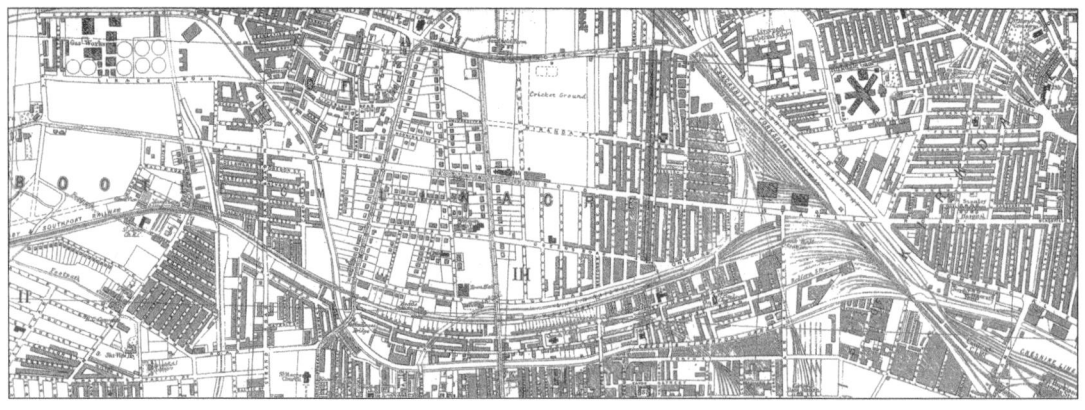

The stretch of Stanley Road shown on a late nineteenth-century map.

AN UNFORTUNATE HURRY

A look towards the scene of the tragedy.

The court heard that the fatal firearm belonged to Mr Boyle who often took it away to sea with him for personal defence. He had handed it to his wife only the previous day and he had intended to dispose of the cartridges on the morning in question. As fate would have it, he had been called away in a hurry, and for the first time ever, had forgotten all about the bullets. A jury returned a verdict of death by misadventure and expressed the deepest of sympathies to the remaining members of the Boyle household.

NO. 22 MOUNT PLEASANT

It was the early hours of 12 November 1880 and upon an address in Mount Pleasant lay the eyes of several police officers waiting to launch a stealthy midnight raid. Their visit concerned illegal acts of gambling allegedly taking place at No. 22, a house run by a Mrs Smith. The word was given and Detective Strettell hammered hard upon the door. It was a few cold moments before the officer and his colleague Detective Marsh could make a rush past the weary-eyed landlady and head up the stairs. On the first floor they found three gentlemen along with a selection of articles suggesting that the house was indeed a haven for criminal gaming. There was the tell-tale apparatus of a roulette-wheel carrying case and a number of tickets and papers relating to

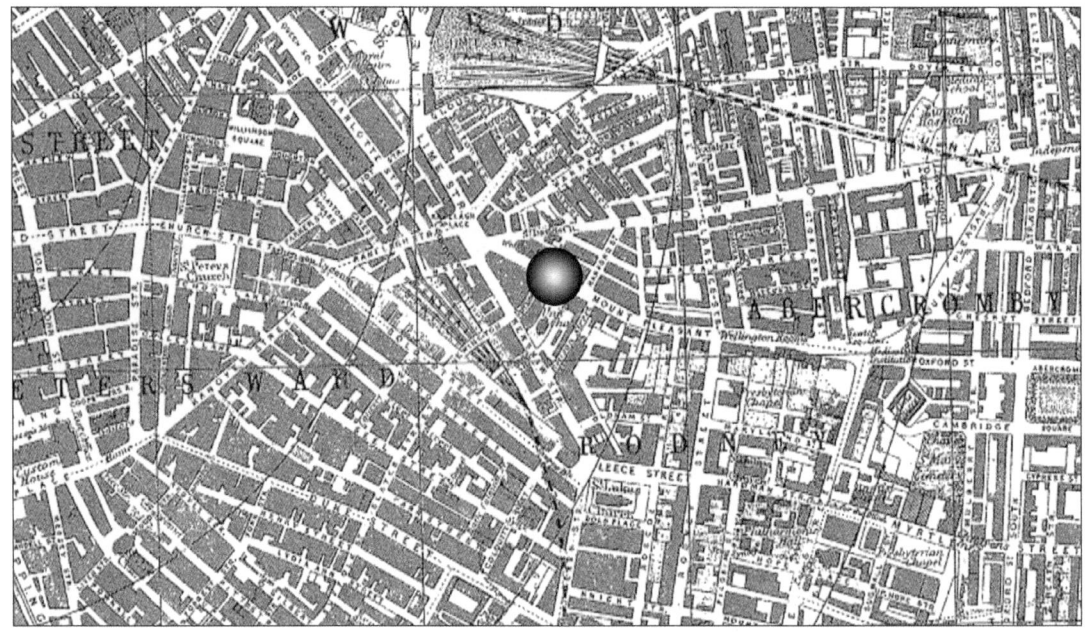

Mount Pleasant, on a map from 1885.

such underworld activities. The three men, who in all rented two rooms in the property, were promptly arrested.

On 20 November at the Dale Street Police Court, the respectfully dressed accused, Joseph Morris, James Smith and Henry Adams, stood trial before stipendiary magistrate Mr Raffles. It was alleged that each of the middle-aged prisoners played their own specific part in the business. One acted as banker, another as croupier and the third acted as a sort of overall manager. Mr Raffles heard how there was a fourth man who had lodged at the house three or four days before the raid, but his purpose, if any, could not be determined.

A body search of the prisoners revealed a mini-library of documents, all of which pointed a paper-based finger of guilt at the three ashen fellows. One was a printed circular and it read:

The West of Scotland Army and Navy Club.
Sir,
My rooms will be opened during the race week at the above address (36 as played at Baden Baden). The honour of your patronage will oblige. Your humble servant, Thomas Maloney. N.B. Play commencing at nine o'clock each evening.

'I suppose as 'used' to be played at Baden Baden?' enquired the magistrate.

'Yes, and there was also a little ticket found in their possession, which is an exact copy of the roulette cloth with '36' on one side, and on the other, 'as played in Baden Baden.' I propose simply this,' said prosecution solicitor Mr Marks, 'that the *onus prolandi* rests with them to show that it is not a common gaming house.'

For the defence Mr Bartlett chose against cross-examining any of the witnesses but instead threw himself entirely at the mercy of the court. Yes, his clients had offended and broken the law, but 22 Mount Pleasant was not a common gaming house within the meaning of the statute. It wasn't fitted up with all kinds of paraphernalia for carrying out gaming and these prisoners were not even local to the town. They had come, as with the hordes of other gamblers, to see the famous races at Aintree. They were merely passing through. 'I trust the bench will take that into consideration and be as merciful and lenient as possible,' pleaded Mr Bartlett.

Mr Raffles said that he did not believe it to be desirable at all to pass lightly over the offence. He stated that he could not think of any place more destructive than a gambling house of that sort, even at the time of the races. 'It is a ruination to young men,' tutted the magistrate, before ruling that each of the men must

The illegal gambling den in Mount Pleasant.

pay £100 plus costs, or face six months in prison with hard labour in default. A woman in the crowd fainted upon hearing the decision of the bench and had to be physically removed from the court. At the request of Mr Marks, the £40 worth of gaming equipment found at the premises was destroyed.

Later, Mr Raffles again had the men brought up to the dock. He stated that he had discovered that under the summary jurisdiction act the highest term of imprisonment he could enforce for anything over £20 was three months. With this in mind an alternative term of incarceration was set to three months.

In addition Richard Tudor, a publican living in Cardiff, was summoned for being the proprietor and occupier of the building in question. Mr Raffles was informed that the defendant took the two rooms and agreed to a rent of £4 10s a week. The detectives Strettell and Marsh gave evidence in support and Mr Tudor was subsequently issued with a £100 fine and costs, or three months in default.

NURSE JONES

Shell shock, the illness which can drive men insane, is characterised by numerous mental complaints. It was an awful, yet sadly commonplace, side-effect of the First World War. Between 1914 and 1918 the British Army identified 80,000 men under its control. Symptoms included tiredness, irritability, giddiness, a lack of concentration and crushing headaches which led to many a soldier's breakdown.

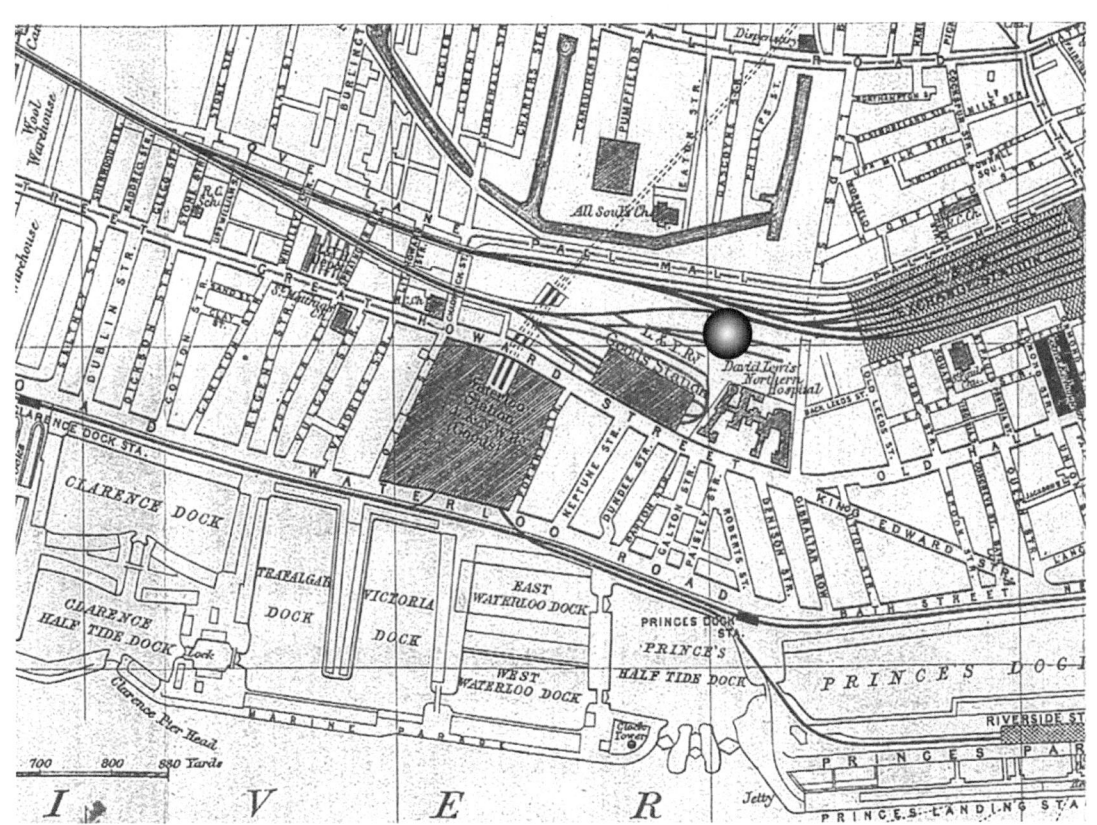

The David Lewis Northern Hospital as shown on a map from 1924.

The junction of Great Howard Street and Leeds Street where the hospital once stood.

Alice Kate Jones was a nurse at the David Lewis Northern Hospital in Great Howard Street. She had been a dedicated member of the nursing profession for two years, and now, at the age of twenty-six, was blossoming into a confident, capable and above all caring member of staff.

In November 1918, Alice took some leave at her family home in Rochdale. Over dinner she happened to mention to her father Robert details about a patient who had recently come into her care. Joseph Hutty was a twenty-five-year-old soldier who had suffered greatly from the recent war. As a member of the Canadian Expeditionary Force he had been posted to fight in France and had since become an invalid with tremendous difficulty walking. Joseph was of course Canadian and therefore had no friends or family in the area. Miss Jones asked her father if he had any objections to Mr Hutty coming to stay with them for a while as she thought he would benefit from the company. Mr Jones could see no harm in the idea, and as long as he did not have to do anything, Mr Hutty could come and stay for a short time at the house.

The David Lewis Northern Hospital as seen in 1902.

Soon afterwards, Joseph was brought to Rochdale to aid his recovery, with Nurse Jones on hand to help. As Alice had predicted, the week-long break did do the Canadian a world of good and the man left in much better shape than when he first arrived. Alice also seemed quite taken with the former man in uniform.

'I will make it up with Kitty,' said Joseph, as he had a quiet word with her father.

Seeing the romantic glint in Joseph's eye, Mr Jones advised his house guest to wait until Alice had finished her training and until he had found himself a job. Mr Hutty agreed and on good terms he left Rochdale, and Alice, and headed to America. The following months saw the soldier write to his intended in an attempt to entice her affection, and it seemed his words were working.

However, in February 1919 Alice replied to one of his letters with the shattering news that she was not sure if there was now anything between them – and that it would be best if they were nothing more than friends.

In consequence of Alice's change of heart Joseph wrote to her sister, Elsie, saying that he had come back from America to try and get Kitty back in his arms, and even though his visit may not prove to be of any use, he had to try.

Elsie contacted her sister and informed her of the message she had received. She was compelled to reply:

July 16, 1919,

Dear Joe,
It pains me very much to have to write you this. Whatever made you come back to England again? Surely you must have understood my decision, and you might have known that I never change my mind. It is completely made up. To be as we were before can never be. I do not love you, and it is far better that we should not see each other again. You say that you love me, but it's probably merely infatuation on your part. For old time's sake let my decision be final and please prove yourself a man by accepting my decision. If you really love me I am very sorry Joe. It will be hard for you, but time is a wonderful healer. Some day you will meet somebody who will make you happy, which I could never do. My whole thoughts are in my work and I am very happy.

Joseph's heart ached upon reading the words. It was as if his life had become worthless. He had survived the war, but this onslaught on his emotions seemed too much to take.

July 17, 1919,

Dear Kitty,
Your letter has proved too much for me, so I am ending this misery. You can have the gratification of costing one man's life. It is impossible to pull myself together. I love you with all my heart and I could hardly believe that you would have turned me down without seeing me for once. I believe you loved me until I went away. If my mother writes to you or your people, let her know what has happened to me. I will say good bye for now.

The following week on 23 July, Miss Jones travelled to Rochdale to meet with her father. She told him that Mr Hutty was constantly writing to her and harassing her. It was clear that she was not interested and only viewed her relationship with her former patient as platonic, if that.

'I have written to Joseph refusing to meet him. I also told him of Captain Schoo,' added Alice.

The next day Joseph, who was still very much alive, visited the Northern Hospital with his friend Charles McMahon. Charles had been acquainted with Hutty for some time and in recent days had accompanied him on other rose-tinted visits to the establishment. On one occasion Charles overheard a conversation between his companion and a porter boy, during which Joe showed the lad several photographs. On coming to a cabinet card of Alice Jones, he heard him remark, 'that is my girl.' Now the American found himself yet again at the hospital with his friend, who was yet again pestering the porters. 'Do you know what Nurse Jones was wearing when she went out?' asked Hutty. He seemed more agitated than usual and was most keen to find out the woman's whereabouts. The porter did not know if Alice had even started her shift yet. Joseph sighed and left the hospital to wait outside.

Charles sat on a wall as his pal paced up and down the street hoping that Nurse Alice would soon appear to begin work.

Meanwhile, in Exchange Street, Alice had just disembarked from the ten-thirty locomotive from Rochdale and was eager to meet Frank Schoo. He was also a former patient of Alice's who had been placed under her care owing to a fractured foot. In appreciation of their help, Mr Schoo had taken Alice and another nurse to the theatre on several occasions and the pair had become well acquainted. That evening the two walked slowly along the bleak but busy streets to the hospital chatting merrily along the way. On approaching the steps to the nurse's workplace, Joseph Hutty advanced towards them.

'Nurse Jones?' he said.

Four quick flashes illuminated the hospital forecourt, each with its own hideous and unmistakable resonance. Alice fell back onto the blood-splattered steps before a further three bullets were sent flying into her flesh at almost point-blank range. Under a cloak of screams, Hutty ran from the scene, totally insane.

Colleagues rushed to save Nurse Jones but death had been practically instantaneous. All seven bullets had entered her body, causing fatal injuries with no hope of medical salvation.

'Yes I shot her. I only hope she is dead,' said Hutty as he was handcuffed in the Bridewell. He alleged that the dead woman had given him a certain disease and pointed to the dark marks that covered the lower part of his face. Following the inquest, which found Joseph guilty of wilful murder, a trial at the assizes was ordered for 5 November.

Dr Evans of the Northern Hospital told the coroner that the body of the deceased had suffered a number of bullet wounds. Her organs were all in a perfectly healthy condition and Alice had suffered from no disease whatsoever.

When questioned about the alleged disease Mr Hutty was suffering from, Dr Ashcroft stated that every possible test had been made as a consequence of his allegation, and not one result came back positive.

Frank Schoo, a chief officer on an American ship, was next to take the stand.

'Were you very friendly with Miss Jones?' asked Mr Madden with raised eyebrows.

'No, we were just good friends; that's all. She was very good to me while I was in hospital.'

At Mr Madden's request the letters which the prisoner and the deceased had written were read to the court. One of them he sent to her included the phrase 'have a heart and come to your laddie', and referred to a position which he had obtained. In a later letter Joseph asked whether Alice had received an order for fifty dollars which was for the purchasing of an engagement ring.

Hutty elected to give his own evidence and he approached the stand with some difficulty.

'I had been invalided out of the Army through shell shock. Soon after meeting Nurse Jones I began to walk out with her and eventually we became engaged,' Joseph said.

He continued to speak of his relationship with the deceased, saying that he was a Catholic but his fiancée was of another faith. Apparently Alice was willing to convert and turn to Catholicism so that they could be together and go off to marry in America. Subsequently he said that he had later received a letter informing him of Alice's new decision to break off all contact and to carry on with her work.

'Were you deeply in love with the woman at the time?' posed Mr Madden.

At this, Joseph Hutty began to cry and sobbed wildly in the box. It was several minutes before he could continue and even then his evidence could only be given in broken sentences.

In answer to Mr Madden Hutty said that arrangements for their marriage were so far advanced he had seriously considered sending out an order for two hundred and fifty dollars to Miss Jones to pay for her passage out to the States. He also spoke of how one occasion when Alice had written to him detailing an incident that happened in New Brighton, to the effect that a man had been annoying her and would not believe she was engaged. 'It was then that she requested I send her a ring,' supplemented the prisoner.

It was heard that Joseph had suffered another shock while working in America and this explosion had somewhat maddened his old complaint. He had only returned to England to see if the matters between himself and the deceased could be straightened out. Joseph emphatically denied that his intention was to come and take away the life of Nurse Jones. The revolver, he said, was a souvenir from France, and it was true that during his previous attempts to meet with the deceased he had never carried it upon his person. Normally the weapon was kept in a portmanteau, but he had taken it with him that day because of news that there had been trouble at the American Bar where a man had been assaulted and robbed.

'Then although you went out on several occasions, you never carried the revolver until the day of the tragedy?' asked Mr Madden.

'That is so,' replied Hutty, who also admitted that he had taken to drinking heavily for several days prior to the killing.

The Canadian again broke down when asked for his recollection of that momentous evening. Through tears he answered incoherently that he had seen a woman who he took to be Nurse Jones coming along the street with another man. 'I was not sure that it was her so I went up to them to inquire. I asked her name, and she answered me,' sobbed Joseph. 'I pulled out my gun and saw the flash of the shots and heard the reports. I do not know how many shots I fired. I thought, "I am killing her, and I cannot stop."'

Evidence was given to the prisoner's state of mind. Dr Nelson had previously had Hutty under observation and remarked that his shell shock was of the worst kind he had ever dealt with.

Dr Clarke had recently examined the prisoner. It was his view that if Hutty was himself a victim, a victim of unrequited love, he was a man likely to lose all control and act on sheer impulse. He did not, however, say that the prisoner was actually insane at the time of the tragedy.

Mr Madden for the defence addressed the jury. 'I am not putting before you the theory of insanity, but of irresistible impulse. If ever a man loved a woman this man did.' He contended that if his client had set out to murder the girl he would have taken the gun the previous day when he went to the hospital with the intention of demanding an explanation. 'Love,' said Mr Madden, 'robbed a man of his reason and of his power of action. It led to great joys; it also led to great sorrows. It is an allurer, a fascinator, a seducer leading to either a feast of joy or a dance of death!'

Mr Madden implored the jury to agree with the opinion of Dr Clarke, that Joseph Hutty fired the gun through irresistible impulse alone. His client ought not to pay the full penalty of the law.

Guilt was soon decided upon by the jury and a verdict of wilful murder was duly delivered. Hutty's death was scheduled for 25 November leaving just under three weeks for any pleas for mercy to be met. A petition of reprieve was organised immediately and an amazing 34,000 signatures were collected from both sides of the Atlantic. The Home Secretary Edward Shortt evaluated the fragile circumstances and felt warranted in advising King George V to commute the prisoner's sentence to one of life imprisonment.

Love is indeed, a powerful force.

INDEX

Adams, Henry 117
Addison Street 73
Alcide, Adline 114
Alexander, Detective Sergeant 109
Alsop, James Wilcox 44
Ashcroft, Charlotte 99
Ashcroft, Henry 100
Aspinall, Clarke 74
Aspinall, Mr 114
Atkinson, Mr 81
Avory, Mr Justice 86

Bailey, Detective Sergeant 41
Banfield Terrace 87
Bankfield Crescent 87
Barnes, Dr 46
Bartlett, Mr 117
Basnett Street 22
Bath Street 103
Beamish, Dr 95
Bell, Police Constable 34
Benson, Police Constable 55
Bibby, Ellen 62
Bibby, Mary 62
Blackburn, Mr Justice 35
Boyle, John 114
Brannigan, Margaret 27
Brannigan, Peter 26, 28
Brennan, Mary 97
Bridge Street 10
Briggs, Dr 66
Brighouse, Mr 14
Brogan, Peter 95
Brown Street 26
Brown, John 75
Brown, William 55
Browne, Alexander 14
Browning, Mr 80
Brownlow Hill 101
Brunswick Street 52
Bryom Street 71
Bunnett, Emma 95
Burgess, Mrs 113

Burke, Ann 40
Burlington Street 103

Campbell, George 51
Campbell, Mrs 49
Canevali, John 108
Canevali, Maud 108
Carruthers, Isabella 24
Castle Street 44
Chalmer, Thomas 105
Champman, Dr 66
Charter Street, 67
Chesters, Mrs 93
Chesters, Robert 95
Christian Street 68
Chubb, Charles 60
Clarke, Dr 125
Clitheroe, James 89
Cockburn Street 112
Coleridge, Judge 48
College Road 12
Commins, Dr 75
Connell, Mr 43
Coombes, Ann 78
Cornett, Dr 69
Crowe, Thomas 35

Dale Street, Bridewell 46
Dale Street Police Court 57, 117
Davies, Joseph 12
Dawber, Sarah 77
Day, Mr Justice 75
Dinely, George 51
Dodd 88
Donaldson, Robinson 24
Doubleday, Helen 99
Duckworth, Detective Sergeant 68
Dunnett, Horace 70

East, Dr 86
Eaton Street 61
Eckersley, John 62
Edwards, Thomas 31

Ellis, Dr 73
Embledon Street 94
Erie, Sir William 62
Ernest, Mrs 112
Evans, Dr 123
Evans, Sarah 68
Everton Brow 73
Exchange Street East 45

Faraday, John 83
Faraday, Mary 83
Fitzsimmons, Mrs 93
Forsyth, Mary 24
Foster, Sergeant 15
Fowler, Superintendent 22

Gaskell, Mrs 85
Gavin, Constable 68
Gibson, Jane 37
Gillard, John 94
Godwin Street 92
Gosling, Mr 88
Gradwell, Police Constable 107
Graham, Mrs 101
Gray, Edwards 102
Great Charlotte Street 80
Great Howard Street 46, 60, 120
Green Lane 21
Griffiths, Rose 9

Haines, Police Inspector Stephen 103
Hale, Sub Inspector 73
Harris, Miss 57
Harrison, Magistrate William 23
Haughton, Mr 52
Heathcoat, Mr 103
Higgins, Mr 90
Holloran, Thomas 55
Hope Place 111
Huddleston, Baron 24
Hughes, John 62
Hutchinson, Superintendent 82
Hutty, Joseph 120

INDEX

Ivanhoe Road 16

James, Mr 100
Jameson, Mr 24
Jenkinson, Catherine 94
Jenkinson, Sarah 92
Jones, Alice Kate 120
Jones, Catherine 34
Jones, James 62
Jones, Mr 120
Joyce, Margaret 16

Kemble Street 78
Kilshaw, John 87
King, John 107
Kirkbride, Elizabeth 17
Kirkbride, John 21
Kirkbride, William 23
Kirkpatrick, Jane 73
Kirkpartrick, Maxwell 71
Kneale, Detective Inspector 41
Kynaston, Edward 53

Lamb, Mr 83
Lancaster, Ada 64
Lancelot's Hey 56
Lark Lane 16
Larkin, Dr 65
Lavelle, Michael 71
Lawton, Mr 90
Letitia Street 37
Lewis, William 85
Leyden Street 40
Livingstone, Magistrate 57
Livingstone, George Ramsey 52
Livingstone, Revd Canon 53
Lockwood, Elizabeth 57
Lockwood, Mrs 57
Lockwood, Robert 57
London Road 34

MacDonald, Detective Sergeant 73
Madden, Mr 48, 86, 124
Madge, Mr 51
Manisty, Mr Justice 24
March, Detective 116
Marks, Mr 117
Marmion Road 14, 16
Marsh, John, 85
Martin, Superintendent 20, 99
Mawdsley, William 49
McCormick, Catherine 105
McCrudden, Mary 62
McGeorge, Reginald 14
McKenna, Elize 61

McMahon, Charles 123
Messenger, Mr 82
Metcalf, Police Constable 45
Micklethwaite, Police Constable 34
Morgan, Inspector 111
Morris, Joseph 117
Morrison, Detective Sergeant 94
Moss, Magistrate Sir Thomas 51
Mounsell, Mr 89
Mount Pleasant 116
Mountfield, Detective Sergeant 13
Myers, Thomas 99

Nelson, Dr 125
Nesbitt, Susannah 93
Netherfield Road 96
Nicholson, Isabella 23
Norman Street 31, 32
Norris, Mr 51

O'Brien, Edward 92
O'Brien, Miss 27
O'Feeley, Dr 82
Oliver, Dr 16
Orbeti, Emma, 19
Osborn, Inspector 78
Osborn, Mr E. 64

Page, William 87
Park Road 37, 68
Parker, Ernest 95
Paull, Dr 113
Picton, Mr 80
Piggot, George 94
Pilgrim Street 111
Pitts, Dr Henry Yates 21
Powell, Mary 101
Powell, Mr 102
Prescott Street 46
Price, Sergeant 99
Princess Street 99
Pullard, Eliza 105

Queen Square 80
Quinn, Thomas 28

Raffles, Mr 117
Rawdon, Henry Greenwood 34
Reader, Mr 49
Reed, Police Constable, 23
Richmond Row 72
Roberts, Mr Mills 83
Roberts, William 72
Robinson, Sergeant 18

Rodney Street 65
Rushton, Mr 60

Sampson, Mr 55
Sampson, Mr 64, 68
Sanderson, Mr 47
Sawney Pope Street 73
Schoo, Frank 123
Sheppard, Superintendent 20
Sherridan, John 87
Shortt, Edward 126
Singleton, James 37
Singleton, Mrs 39
Smith, Annie 67
Smith, Dr Kellet 29
Smith, James 117
Smith, Mrs 116
Stanley Road 114
Steward, Magistrate 98
Stewart, Magistrate Mr 43
Stewart, Mr 78
Strettell, Detective 116
Sullivan, Thomas 31
Sutton Street 18

Taylor, Ethel 109
Thomaston Street 96
Tickle, William 75
Tonge, Isabella 31
Torr, Mr 90
Treby, Alfred 39
Tudor, Richard 118

Usher, Mary Jane 26

Vaughan, William Stanley 46

Wallace, Frances 112
Walsh, Inspector 21
Walton, Dr 63
Ward, Frederick 10
Warwick Street 38
Watmough Street 73
Watts, Agnes 67
Wilkins, Mr 63
Wilkins, Sergeant 88
Wilson, Hugh 75
Wilson, James 51
Wilson, Jane 32
Wilson, Mr 39
Willes, Mr Justice 91
Williams, Elizabeth 85
Willis, Mr Justice 26
Woods, Mary 89